A Little One
Amidst the Shadows

by Michael L. McCoy

with illustrations by Anisa L. Baucke

Book 2 in

The Chronicles of Peniel

published by

CHJ Publishing
1103 West Main
Middleton, Idaho, 83644

Text copyright © 1999 by Michael L. McCoy
All rights reserved.

Illustrations copyright © 1999 by Anisa L. Baucke
Used with permission.

Photographs copyright © 1999 by Blaylock Photo Center
Used with permission.

Library of Congress Cataloging-in-Publication Data
99-074763

ISBN 0-927022-41-9

Printed in the United States of America.

Acknowledgments

All thanks and praise to God Who has blessed me with many gifted and dedicated people, and Who has worked through them to get this book in print. For centuries, authors have added their works to the long rows of bookshelves. Many of their writings have made me think, provided me with ideas and guided me in many and various ways. In the following paragraphs I mention representative authors and offer words from their works. Other individuals mentioned, whose pilgrimages on earth continue to date, have been an immense encouragement to me; some by leading and drawing, others by prodding and exhorting, a few by counseling and suggesting, one by walking beside me.

Thanks be to the Holy Spirit for the Bible, the inspired and inerrant Word of God which reveals the historical Good News of Christ Jesus to us, and for bestowing the gift of personal faith to believe such Word of God. Indeed, the Apostle Paul declares that the blessings of God are not earned by good works but rather, are gracious gifts. *If it is the adherents of the law who are to be heirs, faith is null and the promise is void. ... That is why it depends on faith, in order that the promise may rest on grace.*

Romans 4:14, 16

Thanks be to God for pastors and parishioners who stood and proclaimed the truth when called upon to present a defense for the hope that was in them. They confessed that *at every mention of mercy we must remember that this requires faith, which accepts the promise of mercy. Similarly, at every mention of faith we are also thinking of its object, the promised mercy. For faith does not justify or save because it is a good work in itself, but only because it accepts the promised mercy.*

Apology of the Augsburg Confession

Thanks be to the Father of lights for theologians and playwrights like Dorothy Sayers. Having recently re-read her 1939 play, *The Devil to Pay*, there is little doubt that the following quotation from the work had a subconscious influence on me.

FAUSTUS

I stand
Between the devil and the deep seas of God
On a road that leads nowhither. This is strange --
The love of God urges my feet towards hell,
The devil that seeks to have me flings me back
Into God's arms. Are you two allies, then,
Playing into each other's hands, and grinning
Friendship across my frontiers? I will have
The truth of this, although the stink reek up
And blast the airs of Heaven! Thou, Mephistopheles,
Answer again, and this time all the truth,
Art thou God's henchmen or His master? Speak!
Who made thee?

MEPHISTOPHELES
God, as the light makes the shadow.

FAUSTUS
Is God, then, evil?

MEPHISTOPHELES
God is only light,
And in the heart of the light, no shadow standeth,
Nor can I dwell within the light of Heaven
Where God is all.

FAUSTUS
What art thou, Mephistopheles?

MEPHISTOPHELES
I am the price that all things pay for being,
The shadow on the world, thrown by the world
Standing in its own light, which light God is.

Thanks be to the Great Shepherd of the sheep Who has blessed His Church with faithful undershepherds and pastoral dogmaticians like Rev. Tim Pauls. On several occasions Pastor Pauls reviewed the manuscript for character development and argument direction. His suggestions for clarity and focus, along with the fraternal demeanor in which he offered them, resulted in chapters and sections being re-written with a willing and glad spirit.

Thanks be to the Author of life for the fine people at CHJ Publishing. Dennis Jones and the rest of his family are hard-working folk who have led me through the publishing process with kindness and know-how. In this time of routine dishonesty, suspicious mistrust and unfulfilled contracts, I note with privileged satisfaction that Clinton Jones and I have neither had, nor required, a signed contract or a notarized agreement. At every point, he and I have promised our word to one another with a handshake and trusted that said promises would be fulfilled.

Thanks be to the Bridegroom for blessing me with my beloved wife and best friend. You would not be reading or hearing this book had it not been for her encouragement and support. Judy has read the manuscript on numerous occasions and made suggestions on wording and sentence structure. Surely the king of Massa had someone like her in mind when the Holy Spirit moved him to write. *Her children rise up and call her blessed; her husband also, and he praises her: "Many women have done excellently, but you surpass them all."*

Proverbs 31:28-29

Finally, an important distinction needs to be made and explained. I am not an author who preaches sermons. Rather, I am a servant of Christ and a steward of God's mysteries who also happens to write a book or two. An important part of that service and stewardship is the proclamation of the Word in sermons. The motivation and way I write and prepare a sermon is the same for this book. In both sermon and book, my sincere desire is to communicate to the hearer and to the reader the objective truth of the Gospel -- of the Good News of Jesus' Incarnation, Life, Death, Resurrection and Ascension. Therefore, this book is very much like one of my sermons. It is neither perfect nor complete. Every parish pastor knows that his sermon "needs work." If he were to wait until he had written the perfect sermon, he would never make a proclamation from the pulpit. The weekly deadline approaches and the people of God are in need of and long to hear the Word of forgiveness, eternal life and salvation. So it also is with this book. If I were to wait until a nearly perfect manuscript had been written, this story would remain in the mind of the writer. While there is no doubt that this book "needs work," the deadline approaches and there are still people who need to hear the Story.

Should any of the errors within this book be a transgression of His will, especially sins of ignorance, then I look to and trust in the Lamb of God Who takes away the sin of the world.

SOLI DEO GLORIA!

To the Reader and the Hearer

The Story is eternal, from everlasting to everlasting, without beginning and without end. Our stories are different. While participating in the everafter, we do have individual starting points in time. The Author of life fully knows each of our stories from before *in the beginning* unto life everlasting; we do not. As we live from day to day we occasionally wonder about the past, we often ask *why* in the present and we are called to hope in the future. The past is when the promise was given. The present is the time of trust in the promises of God. The future, with its due reward, waits for our stories to conclude in this world.

The book in your hands is the story of a little one cast forth upon the ground in this land of thorns and thistles. The story is not comprehensive because, as we know and as has been said, no one except the Story Giver is omniscient. The pages that follow tell of three episodes in the life of a man: one night in the young boy's life, one day in the old man's death and a passion week in between. Although these events in this little one's life unfold in three unnamed locations, this much is certain, the three places are within the borders of the land known as Peniel.

Michael L. McCoy
The Visitation
31 May Anno Domini 1999

TABLE OF CONTENTS

for the little ones

The LORD will rise up as He did at Mount Perazim,
He will rouse Himself as in the Valley of Gibeon --
to do His work, His strange work,
and perform His task, His alien task.

Isaiah 28:21

CHAPTER 1

BIG FEAR

The bedroom had the basics. There were no curtains. Neither mirror nor pictures hung on the dingy white wall. A drawerless nightstand had only a lamp on it. The lamp's pull chain hung down and tapped against the tapered, black walnut shaft. A single, small bed filled the corner. The little one in the bed would not fall out because the mattress and springs sagged in the center. The little one was not asleep. There was always fear, but it was not big fear. Not yet. His eyes looked to the center of the room and not to the wooden framed window above the bed.

The sound came first. It always did, like a warning that the other was coming. If the boy's eyes were closed and he had not fallen asleep, the sound caused him to open his eyes as it announced the imminent image on the wall. There was sound, but at first it was not big sound. Light came and was cast on the wall at the foot of the bed. In the first moments of its existence the paneled light remained in place. The sound was not so important at this point. The first sound served to announce the advent of the paned light. Slowly the four-paned image clarified and began drifting to the opposite corner of the room. As it shaped itself around the inside corner of the small room, it picked up speed along the adjacent wall. Suddenly the grating sound came and the picture leaped across the open doorway leading to the hall. In that instant had anyone or anything been standing in the doorway that one or that thing would have been illuminated.

No matter how often the light came, and it did come often, the boy's eyes remained fixed on the opening. Like a flashbulb capturing a still image, the scene of the entryway was inscribed on his mind. He hoped no one was standing in the doorway but the little boy always had to watch. That look, however short, was always too long. The traveling panes of light disappeared before his eyes darted from the door. The experience never failed to frighten the boy. Yet it was not the big fear that would cause him to cry out for his mother.

Darkness and sound always accompanied the critical moment. In the midst of the shadows, the first sound varied not only from the beginning of the event to the end, but also from incident to incident. Once in a while the sound was quite small, undetected until the louder grating noise came and the framed lights jumped across the doorway. Just as often the sound was big, but since it always began at a distant point and gradually increased, it did not cause big fear. If there had been no sounds it would have puzzled the boy, but of course, this never happened. In reality, the sounds were not threatening in themselves since big fear was triggered by the visual. The sounds simply announced the coming of the light in the darkness.

At night, while in bed, complete light or total darkness did not scare the boy. A combination of the two, particularly when the darkness prevailed, provided a setting for shadows and a prelude for panic. Darkness was invariably a part of the scene when the phenomenon took place. Without the darkness the vision never appeared. Without the light in the darkness of this world's night, the boy could only wonder if anyone stood in the doorway. Though he feared the light, he needed it to reassure himself that he was alone. While he did not want anyone to be standing in the doorway, he did require the assurance that no one was there.

It is true that a certain amount of natural light came into the room through the window at the boy's back. However, the moonlight was never enough to give that doorway any distinct detail. The doorway was away from the window and did not receive sufficient moonbeams for the boy to be sure. As if planned or permitted, the moonlight only engaged an already active imagination. The weak light eliminated total darkness and created shadows. The boy could only imagine what creatures had assumed the shape of those shadows and were lurking about the room waiting to get him. But that did not create big fear because there would always be doubt that they were anything other than shadows. The little one in the bed needed a flash of light across the doorway to be sure that no one was there.

The boy never looked out the window situated behind him and above his bed. The paned-glass window was behind him because the boy always reclined on his right side. The awful window threatened him. Not only would anyone outside the panes of glass be too close if the boy did look, but a stranger's facial features would be hidden in the shadows. As such, even if it were his mother looking in, he could not have recognized her. Of course, his mother would never do such a thing. Just the thought of looking out the window put him on the verge of big fear. The boy did not think about casting such a foolish glance.

His eyes remained fixed on the doorway. Who might be the one standing in the doorway? The boy knew his mother was not the one there. She never entered the room without announcing herself. Besides, even before she ever entered his room, he knew she was coming. Before she got to the doorway, her padded, familiar footsteps would be heard in the hall. The little one always knew his mommy's walk. Daddy would not be the one standing in the doorway. Daddy was not home. He never was. No indeed, the one standing in the entryway was always the nameless Other. It might have been a bad man, or a god, or a spirit, or a monster, or even the devil, but it was always Other. That's what the little one knew and believed. Just thinking about the Other put him on the brink of big fear. He didn't like to think about this, but he always thought about this.

If the boy had just been put to bed and was not sleepy, he imagined being a soldier behind enemy lines and in hiding. The covers were pulled above his nose. At such times, the pillow on top of his head served as concealed covering. Only his eyes peered from his protection. Footsteps and voices of searching enemy soldiers froze the little one in place. The pretend enemy never located him, though often they came quite near, sometimes even standing or resting near his hiding place. On occasion he hid under a net of camouflaged leaves. Usually he was hidden in a dirt cave just big enough for his body. At times, he could even feel the heat from the campfire of the enemies. The boy's enemies were completely frustrated in their attempts to locate the intruder. Of course, the little one could not understand the language of the soldiers. No doubt it was some foreign language or some secret code. He never needed to understand it. Let them scheme, he thought, they would not discover him. But remember, these men were never allowed to use a tank or a truck. Why? Because it would not be fair. Besides, that sort of noise from a vehicle was too much like the sound which announced the coming light. If he permitted the enemy to drive a rig, the imaginary game would come to an immediate end. That is one way that the war games might end. Usually the games ended when the boy fell asleep hiding in his earth cave.

The boy tried never to dream about his shadowy room, the outside sounds, the light on the wall or the presence of the Other in the portal. Having such a nightmare would bring big fear as well as a trembling cry for his mother.

His mother was one of the special mothers. There was no one else like her in the entire world. She never forced him to stay in bed by shutting the door or telling him there was a horrid monster under his bed. She did not use coercion, bribery, rewards or the fear of punishment to keep him in bed. She let him know that if he was afraid or if he had a bad dream, all he had to do was call to her and she would come to him. The boy knew he was expected to stay in bed, but also that he could call out for his mother at any time. He believed and trusted in her promise.

Sometimes sleep did not come so quickly and the boy could not occupy his thoughts with the feeble attempts of approaching enemy infantrymen. So, he would hide in the still shadows of the night. At such times, with little eyes peering out of his flannel cocoon and staring into the darkness of the night, he watched the still, murky, obscure silhouettes. On occasion, the sound came and the eyes of the little one opened to full life and flashed to the wall in his room. He was ready when the panels of light slowly drifted to and suddenly raced across the doorway. An instantaneous check was always recorded to make certain no one stood in the doorway.

Once within a time, in that time during this world's night, a time after having foiled some outlaws on horses, the little one stared at the base of the wooden lamp and the pull-chain that hung from the top fixture. The round base, like the tapered shaft, was made of black walnut. The boy knew it was smooth for he had often felt it. Like the shaft, the base was not varnished. Under the base was a round piece of green felt. This pad was glued in place. However, this particular night he did not check it to make certain. He was too tired. Besides he did not want to move around too much. Doing so might have drawn the attention of the Other, and the Other might be standing in the doorway mulling the possibility that this dark room contained a little boy.

So in that moment, when one is neither awake nor asleep, the little one heard the small, soft, grating sound in the distance outside his window. Instantly his eyes opened wide. They dilated in response, focused intently and reflected a concentration of his mind. Without looking he knew the noise was not that of a truck. The distant sound did not grate enough to be a larger vehicle. A car did and a car it was. He shrunk farther from the window at his back and watched across the room. The usual spot reflected from the wall where the light shone. A brilliant white on the wall indicated the high beam of the car's headlights. That night the headlights were dim and the boy looked at the opposite wall with trained eyes and keen attention. He tensed after drawing a preparatory breath. He held it tightly as his pulse increased and his heart pounded.

The paneled light of the cross-pieced, wooden window frame began to grow slightly in brightness and commenced its gradual slide to the corner. The grating sound increased but was rightly ignored by the boy. The image was etched in his memory. The light warped itself around the inside of the corner. At the instant the grating noise peaked, just as the car's front tires twisted on the gravel road to turn the corner in front of his house, the light jumped across the doorway. A surge of brilliant light flooded the doorway. The snapshot was taken and the image of the entryway was sent to his mind. And on this night, unlike all other nights in his short life, the little one had big fear.

2

CHAPTER 2

THIS ONE AND THAT ONE

With no warning of his arrival, he was directly in front of me. One moment I had been straining my eyes to focus on a figure across the creek, and the next instant he was in my face. I say *he* because I sensed a *he*. A dark, hooded cloak hid the features of his face. His probing, piercing eyes, though still hidden from my sight by the early evening shade and the shadows of his hood, looked beyond the surface and penetrated to my soul, if indeed, that sort of invasion is possible. Certainly such a feeling is. His *he-ness* descended upon me like a thick pall and his *other-ness* repelled me. My feet were anchored to the floor of the cabin sill. His closeness was overwhelming and my awareness of him was limited to a featureless face under a dark hood.

The human reactions that accompany such big fear take place instantly and simultaneously. If described with words like "pure terror," they emerge with neither the magnitude nor the intensity necessary to convey what occurred within my body, mind and soul. Like the black characters on this page, such phrases are two-dimensional chains of letters without sufficient depth or dimension. Descriptive words like frightening, horrifying or stunning are thin, anemic and unsubstantial. This inability results from the attempt to depict in words what one has experienced in deed. It is the attempt to capture the grandeur of a roaring, pounding surf, or the still, breathtaking awe of a mountain's lofty peak, or the quiet majesty of a stained glass, cathedral window with a color snapshot. Volumes could be written on the pains of childbirth, all falling woefully short of conveying the experience.

Thus, I confess the pages that follow to be puny and I admit my inability to convey an accurate and true expression of the experience at hand and those events that followed.

Raw, unprocessed terror is the natural reaction of the mind when confronted with instant, horrible dread. Physical responses take place without prompting. One of my primary default actions was vocal. It was not a scream that would require formation by the mouth, but rather a base, primal bellow that originated from the deepest recesses of the lungs, was forced from among the dregs of the stomach and given unrestrained course through the vocal cords, throat and mouth. Accompanied hormones produced by the body sped through my system. My heart experienced the integral of acceleration and jerked to a rate three times normal. My temples pounded. The breathing cycle increased as the lungs lifted the chest. With sweat surfacing, hairs standing on end, eyes dilating instantly, I raised one arm to ward off a blow and to shield my eyes from him. My legs bent as if to prepare for fight or flight. Physically, I was capable of neither.

What mental reactions did I have? These are even more difficult to put into words because such big fear does not lend itself to thinking in words. Pure thought and basic instinct are engaged without prompting. Only later, in the shortest definition of that time period, did I think of the possibilities. However, considering all of them and commencing a course of action are quite different. If my will were capable of being carried out, I would have fled. I willed to be away from this person. But what I willed I could not do. For what seemed an eternity, I stood there hypnotized by the *other-ness* from him. While not a word was spoken between us, he mesmerized me. He had captured me. Had the other one not interceded for me I would have remained completely under the power of the confronter that evening.

Would I have struck him? Of course, that would have been a secondary reaction, one not especially an option considering how I was spellbound by this one standing before me. Would I have struck him? This is difficult to answer. Certainly he deserved a beating, having jumped from nowhere and confronted me as he did. He was someone looking for trouble, lurking about the shadows in dark clothing and appearing as I blinked my eyes. Would I have struck him? I am capable of such, though I have lived a life that has leaned away from such violence. Certainly I would have been justified in bloodying his nose, if indeed, he had a nose. Please recall that because of his hood, I never saw his face. His loose, dark clothing also prevented me from determining the presence of a weapon. He could easily have been hiding a dagger, waiting to kill me the moment I turned to flee. I had no opportunity to assess him. He might have been a military type who would have made short work of me. Or, he could have been much weaker and easily taken down. Would I have struck him? Yes, he intended to place himself directly in front of me and considering his immediate confrontation and the circumstances, I believe I would have been justified.

Would I have killed him? But you ask a hypothetical question, one speculating on what did not happen. Such a theoretical discussion would take us further from what actually took place that evening. You need to hear, not of the possibilities, but of the reality. Therefore, permit me to go back a bit.

The woman, the boy and I were going to rough it in a primitive cabin for a short vacation. After working all day Wednesday, we spent the late afternoon and early evening packing the truck and preparing to leave. We slept until midnight, though the excited boy claimed not to have slept at all. We began Thursday, the 14th, the day of preparation, with the eleven-hour drive to the trail head. We planned to make full use of our Friday vacation day at the camp. Our stay in the mountains would last three days -- too short a time for the seven-year-old boy and too long for his beautiful mother. An acquaintance had offered the use of the rustic cabin and the woman and I gladly seized the opportunity to enjoy several spring days with the boy in the northern mountains. Leaving our vehicle where the gravel road ended and bearing the packs filled with food for three days, we began the nine-mile walk to the remote camp. We started hiking about 1:30 in the afternoon and planned to have this challenging part of our journey completed before 5:30 that evening.

We noticed the steady climb not only from the physical exertion but also in the natural display of changing scenery. The broad leaves of the maples and dense underbrush in the protected lower areas gave way to the hearty evergreens and scattered bushes. At the end of the hike we arrived at the timberline.

The cabin faced a small creek and an impressive stand of noble evergreens protected it from the full force of mountain winds. The primitive cabin was a nostalgic shelter to me, an awesome fortress for the boy and an archaeological ruin to the woman. The back room served as a kitchen, though without piped water. The focal point of the crude kitchen was a rusty stove. It served as the center of attention during the cold evenings and nights. In the morning, coffee water could be heated on it if wood had been collected the previous day. A crude bench and two chunks of wood provided places for sojourners to sit. The stovepipe, bearing rust stains from a leaky roof, disappeared into the dark hole of the kitchen ceiling. The cup board was cupless. Two planks running the length of one wall served as a table and provided a place away from the mice. As long as one stood, it accomplished its intended purposes. Halfway down its length, black bits of wick, spattered wax and a scattering of candle stubs testified to the lack of electricity.

The area above the kitchen originally had been designed as a loft for sleeping and food storage. No straw mattress remained on the wooden plank floor and no food hung from the rafters awaiting a traveler. Loose combustibles had been used for kindling fires. At the center of the loft, the stovepipe emerged from below the floor and ascended through the rough, cedar shake roof. The boy earnestly desired to eat his last meal of the day in this upper room, and so he did. The sloped sides of the loft dictated a stooped posture while standing. The rough evergreen poles used as rafters bowed noticeably, testifying to winters of heavy snow.

Awareness of one's surrounding and caution prevented punctures from exposed shake nails in the roof or spiked knots on the poles. The loft had no railing to protect against falling. The plank floor was large enough for the three sleeping bags we carried. The woman put the boy's bag on the floor between the stovepipe and the gable end of the upper room. She hoped this would keep him from rolling over the edge. She preferred risking a slight burn from a warm stovepipe to an eight-foot fall. Ladder rungs nailed to exposed studs provided access to the loft. Evidently, previous visitors needed the bottom rung for a fire. Now, with the first rung nearly three feet from the earth floor, the woman and I strained at the pull while the boy welcomed the obstacle.

The decision to sleep in the loft was unanimous. The woman chose it because of the warmth coming from the kitchen below and the stovepipe in the loft. In addition, she was pleased with the assurance that any animals snooping around would not be able to climb the ladder, or at least wolves and coyotes could not manage the rungs. Besides, this was the only room in the small structure with a wooden floor. I situated my sleeping bag near the edge of the loft, facing the open doorway below. The boy decided the loft would give us the advantage should rustlers or other bad men enter the cabin. We could, as he reckoned, "descend upon the bandits from above as they were dividing up the loot or plotting some evil scheme." I told him that he might have to do this by himself as my swooping and descending days were confined to memories of what once was. I told the boy to be careful because the intruders might be enemy soldiers who talked in a strange, foreign language, or maybe even communicated in some secret, diabolical code. He thanked me, giving assurance that he would be extra cautious and protect me no matter what happened. I thanked him.

The open area in the front half of the structure provided shelter for animals; probably horses, pack mules or a combination of said beasts. Two stalls had been constructed on each side of the open room. The carpenters had nailed arm-sized branches to the studs to serve as rails for a rope or reins to secure an animal. Only the nails remained, bearing witness to the need for firewood. It did not seem to matter any longer as beasts of burden had not occupied the stalls for years. The wide doorway would have allowed either a saddled horse or a packed mule to enter the stable area without hindrance. The remnants of the wide door leaned lengthwise against the outside wall. The bottom board of the wall, in an advanced stage of decay, was nearly buried with fine, glacial dust and tinder-dry fir needles. A rusted hinge on the siding and a two-by-four threshold endured in their original positions.

I stood on this plank portal that early evening gazing into the darkened woods. With the light supper finished, the woman and the boy sat quietly in the kitchen area. I slowly rocked on the wooden sill as I stared into the darkness and listened to the night. The only sound came from the gurgling trickle of the creek, now nearly dry from the stingy glaciers above. The trail on the other side of the small stream paralleled a line of evergreens. Light came from the western sky, reflected from the gray glacial till and cast vague shadows throughout the wooded area.

As darkness overtook the sunless firmament, the shapes and shadows fused and blended with the gray background. My eyes, deceived in such diminishing light, perceived outlines of gross creatures and my mind imagined slow movements of this conjuring. These ghosts of the imagination all disappeared in the moments I stood gazing. All that is, except for one, a vertical shape that retained its form while being a shade lighter than the dark wooded background.

At first, the shape seemed to float and not move at all, thus causing doubt about its reality and questions concerning my observation of it. After a few moments I detected a horizontal movement and concluded that, whatever it might be, it must be on the trail. Since it came directly at me, it appeared to be still and hovering. As the trail turned and headed in the direction of the summit and, as the creature followed the oblique path, shadowy movements were detected. At this distance and in that darkness I could only see the being when I didn't look directly at it. Moments passed. I discerned that it walked upright and my mind conjured up a bear but rejected that possibility since no bear would walk upright for that distance. I thought of the mysterious Sasquatch and had no basis for eliminating it as a possibility. Nevertheless, since it appeared to be human, I determined it must be human. The thought of his coming to the old cabin increased my anxiety.

I stood still, hoping he would pass by without noticing me. I willed that the woman and the boy would remain quiet and stay in the primitive kitchen. Did the rays from the kitchen candle reach into the darkness allowing him to see them? I would not turn around to check. It no longer mattered. Besides, I wanted to keep my focus on this suspect man. If I glanced away, I might never locate the intruder again, especially in the increasing darkness. I guessed him to be a hundred yards away and still on the trail.

He continued his approach. For short moments he would disappear as he stepped into the varying obscurities of successive shadows. During those brief moments when he was hidden, my eyes strained, looking and searching for the shady man in the shadows. With increasing difficulty, I remained still and focused my attention on the places whence he might emerge.

With every fiber of my being, attention and consciousness trained upon this one in the distance, the other one stepped in front of me. People say that at times of such confrontation, or at the sudden prospect of impending death, an entire life flashes by. For me, after the instantaneous reaction of terror when confronted by this hooded man and as the stupor caused by the shock began to subside, the possible scenarios automatically came to the forefront of my mind.

I had been taken in by a clever deception. The one far away stole my attention while the nearer one slithered in from the side. How foolish I had been! One lured me to him while the other closed in from the flank. One desiring to be seen from a distance was dressed in lighter clothing while the stealthy one approached in a soiled garment. How was I so certain only two were involved? Even now a third or a fourth could be prowling outside the kitchen and examining the outside walls for an access window or door. The woman and the boy might be in danger. Perhaps they were already bound and gagged. Is that why they made no sound? Were they still alive or had they already fallen victim to these bloodthirsty villains? Is this why I had not heard them since the first one came into view? Was there a back door to this building after all? I didn't recall one but perhaps I had missed it. I should have barred that back door. Maybe there is a fifth one sneaking up behind me at this very moment. I could be unconscious before I finished this thought. What did this band of crooked, thieving, murderers want? I had some money but not much. Is it possible that they would take what money we had and let us go? A sixth one may have climbed a rope and gained entry into the loft. He might be preparing to jump down and knock me to the ground. Was there a rope on the outside of the building leading up to a window of the loft? Perhaps I hadn't seen the rope earlier. How stupid of me to leave a rope there. How moronic of me to have been so deceived.

My feet remained in place, not because of a defiant stance on my part but only due to my inability to move. I am not able to recall how long I remained in this paralyzed position. Time must have passed quickly.

The faceless man confronting me was suddenly knocked away. He was assaulted from his right side and his shoulders and body were driven to his left. His hooded head whiplashed to the right and the awful cracking of neck bones sounded in the silence. He fell against the siding striking his forehead on the outside wall. With his entire weight in total free fall, he came down upon the remnants of the old door with a rib-shattering force. As the hooded man went down, I heard the sharp snapping of bones, boards or both. His breath crushed from him, the man choked, gasped and gurgled. Since night was darkest where he fell, those inhuman noises were the only witnesses that he was still alive. No doubt he would have cried and moaned had he been able.

Before me, in the lighter garment, was the man who had come up the trail. The broad-shouldered man stood over me and I couldn't help but be aware of his size as I looked up to him. His robe revealed a muscular bulk. He had focused his might, force, leverage, weight and will against the man confronting me and released a pummeling force that may very well have been lethal. This intercessor had positioned himself where the other one had been, though not nearly as close. This made me feel at greater ease. He let me have my space and was not confronting me as the other man had. I even sensed he wanted me to be comfortable and I was grateful. Perhaps this was the way I wanted it to be and therefore, convinced myself of his genuine concern for me.

His hood was now down. When he had glided along the trail, his hood was up with the tip pointing to the heavens. Had his hood fallen back in the dashing sprint? Or, had he pushed it back from his brow that I might be able to see his face? I opted to believe the latter. His face, while being rugged and sturdy, was without spot or blemish. Light itself seemed to come from him. But how could this be? Perhaps, since he stood farther away from me than the other one, the last light of the evening sky was cast upon his face. It occurred to me that it may have been the same candlelight I had cursed seconds ago. If so, I was now thankful for the illumination from the kitchen candles. The face he projected was serious but non-threatening; it communicated definite concern and care. If there be no misunderstanding, I might even use the word beautiful to describe his face.

These two had not, as I imagined seconds ago, teamed up against me. I convinced myself that there were only two strangers. The woman and the boy were safe. No outside rope led to the loft. The odds of two against one became, in the worse case, one against one against one. I felt better, but only momentarily.

An opposing thought surfaced. Perhaps a bigger and meaner dog had come to take a meal away from the smaller dog. My guard was up again. While clenching my teeth I made an assessment of my resources. The avenues of escape for my loved ones and myself were considered. As I thought about the sort of attacks that might be possible, he spoke.

"The terror in your eyes is evident, my friend. You have nothing to fear, except from that brutal one on the ground."

Though there was no reason to believe him, his voice conveyed a resolute sincerity that calmed me. Still, not being in a frame of mind that was particularly open to trust at this moment, I resolved to give him no reply.

"Friend, your anxiety is sensed. What may be said to assure you of my good intentions for you?"

Silence was still my best recourse. Listening would help me more than speaking. However, his wrath might be kindled against me if I remained quiet and let his question go unanswered. He had demonstrated his terrible strength, skill, stealth and power, as well as his willingness to use them. Determining to answer him and arriving at the proper response were two different matters. The former was decided and while the latter was being considered, he spoke again.

"Look, my friend, you are terrified and rightly so. You do not know what danger has just come your way, or just how close you were to losing your life this night. But please, please be attentive to the one who will tell you what has just happened. Then you may decide about that one there and about this one here; about what has been done for you and who has done it. That you may be at greater ease, more space will be given to you."

He retreated several feet and I confess, it was appreciated. Though his eyes never moved from me, he remained keenly focused on the man he struck. The woman called out from the back asking what was happening and she received my reply. "Stay there, it's okay." In answering her, I reaffirmed my ability to speak. My neck muscles relaxed enough to let my shoulders fall slightly, but only momentarily. He now knew the woman was with me. What of the boy? The pummeled man, though hidden in the shadows of the evening, was still alive and was regaining enough breath to emit spasmodic moans. His quivering groans revealed the pain he was suffering. Uneven, short and shallow breaths were testimony to serious internal injuries. Even as my mind pictured the man on the ground, my eyes never left the one in front of me and I said to him, "I'm listening."

"You are cautious and that is good. But it is not good enough when that one is stalking you. That one goes about like a beast endeavoring to consume his marked prey. Fear that one, my friend. Only minutes ago, when you stood here gazing at this one coming up the trail, that one sought to overcome you, to sift you and to claim you. Since your journey began that one has been pursuing you. You are the prey. But before you were born, that one was being trailed by the same one who raced across the creek this night to thwart an attack on you and prevent your capture. That one is more than clever. Watch and beware."

"It would not appear that I need to beware of him any longer. He has serious injuries."

"Now is when that one is most dangerous. Wounded and suffering, that one is making the most of the situation here. That one has lost another battle, not just here and not just now, but especially in another place and at another time. Despite eventual defeat, that one seeks others to take to the place prepared for that one. Your struggle now begins, friend."

"What do you mean?"

"You feared that one when confronted a few moments ago. Good, very good. But right now, at this very moment, your fear is changing. You are like the moth, irresistibly drawn to the flame by the light and rushing headlong to the fire that burns."

"I am not heartless. Sure I was afraid of him, I still am. But am I not permitted to have compassion on another human being who has been injured as this man has?"

"In this case, no. You are not permitted, and for two reasons. First, you may have compassion but only as long as your mercy is not used by that one to ensnare you. That is where you are heading right now. Compassion is susceptible to exploitation. If compassion is used for the purposes of deception or diversion, especially with what is taking place here, with what is taking place right at this moment, then it is a deadly and final weakness. A convicted murderer will use whatever is necessary, even the compassion of others, to avoid the gallows. That fallen one, whose very nature it is to pursue and conquer will use your sympathy in order to possess you. Those groans summon you and you are listening with your heart. Now is the time to use your head. Once again, this one who has knocked that one aside to protect you is interceding on your behalf, not with physical strength, but with mental discipline. So now, my friend, you must not have mercy and you must have no compassion. Believe me, this counsel is offered for your own welfare."

"Thank you, I think."

My doubtful gratitude was not well-pleasing to him. He inhaled deeply through his nostrils. The corners of his mouth dipped slightly. He filled his lungs to capacity, and replied, "You think?"

Immediately my fear returned. He spoke with a depth and tone that my father would reach when angry or displeased. My reaction as a little boy was neither to talk back nor to back talk. Rather, I sought a way to get away from him and go to a hiding place. Here there was no where to go. Thinking myself to be intelligent and summoning my courage I repeated my answer to him.

"Yes, thank you, I think. How do I know that you were not stalking me and this other man was attempting to be my intercessor? Maybe he was trying to protect me from you. Is it not possible, or even just as likely, that what you have said about him is true of you?"

"Indeed, quite possible and very likely."

I could detect no flash of anger and no hint of having flustered him. Indeed, his appearance remained one of cool perception and he seemed almost pleased with my response.

"You are wiser than what one might expect, but not as perceptive as you think you are. You present an interesting possibility, and no doubt, with time, you would discover its flaws. However, time is what you have the least of here and now. If that one were your rescuer and if this one were your adversary, well, you would be hurt worse than that one is. The truth is, you would be quite dead. Please remember that the one on the ground worked a way to you among the shadows, keeping a presence hidden until suddenly materializing head-on before you. That one is the one who stalked you, intent on an instantaneous confrontation. So, if you are convinced that that one is your intercessor, then why not thank that one for having at least tried?"

He waited as I thought.

"All of this is beyond you, isn't it? These are ways above your ways and thoughts above your thoughts."

I felt rebuked by his words and somewhat guilty at my own ingratitude. After all, he was correct. He could have killed me with a lesser blow than what the other man received. I had the uncomfortable sensation that he knew exactly what my reactions and thoughts were. He was like my mother who could sense my guilt when in her presence. At such times I wanted to get away from her. Now I wanted to get away from him. How might I divert his attention and end the conversation?

"Look, he needs help. Let's get him inside."

As I moved to locate the injured man amidst the shadows and assist him, the other man shifted his stance to block me.

"Look, I only want to help him get into the shelter."

He expressed his reluctance, "Do you not know that you should not let one like him cross the threshold of your house?"

I was becoming further irritated and replied, "This is not my house. Let's get him inside where we can help him."

"Alright, but you go in and reassure the woman and the boy. I will move that one into the first stall. You need to go into the kitchen and let the woman know what has happened here. If you want to show compassion, you should start with her. She is frightened and she needs you."

While my first reaction to the intercessor's handling of the injured man was apprehension, I realized that strength and quickness in moving the man would be needed. If getting him inside were my task, it would have taken longer and the injured man would have certainly endured greater pain. This, combined with concern for the woman and the boy, made me turn away from the two strangers. While walking to the kitchen, I envisioned the wounded man being jacked from the ground, roughly dragged into the building and callously dumped into a stall. I commanded, "Be careful with him."

"Right," he answered in a tone of mocking concern.

As I spoke with the two in the kitchen, my ears listened to what was happening behind me. Guttural moans surfaced from his throat. Wrenching breaths taken through clenched teeth forced me to look back into the stable area. The candlelight spoiled my night eyes and I saw nothing. I relied on my hearing. A final, heavy thump preceded a single, gasping cry of pain, and then, silence. He either passed out from the pain or was dead. God is merciful and I muttered a prayer of gratitude. A peculiar thought entered my mind. I just thanked someone. Who was it I had thanked? Was it the one in the next room? If so, which one? Quite a silly thought, I mused.

After a few minutes with the others, I returned into the darkness of the outer room. Two steps put me in front of the healthy man. He blocked my way to the injured man.

The intercessor announced, "He is in the first stall. His arms are secured to the rail with a tether."

As if reading my mind, his entire attitude changed. "Listen. You can hear breathing."

Although he was correct, my look was one of disgust. So he continued in a winsome manner, "My friend, you are, of course, quite right. Look, that one is not going anywhere for awhile. This one will take care of that one."

The way he said that he would take care of the injured man left me with no little doubt. Would the man be alive in the morning

32

because the intercessor had taken care of him, or would he be dead for the same reason? I was regaining my full faculties and composure, and beginning to think things through more clearly. If somebody is going to be hurt and die, it is better that it is not myself, the woman or the boy.

Again, as if he knew what I was thinking, he replied, "You go ahead and get your family to bed for the night. Indeed, my friend, please see to the needs of the woman and the boy."

Another thought occurred to me. How did he know about the boy? I had only called to the woman. He must have seen the boy when my back was to the kitchen. That's what I wanted to think, so that's what I thought.

"I'll find a candle so that you have some light to determine how serious his injuries are."

"That is not needed. That one will be cared for. There is not much that one can do this night. You really need to be with the woman and the boy. Things will be better in the morning for all. Rest is called for this night. Needs will be met."

While I was not completely satisfied with the situation, his voice carried a note of concern for the man as well as for me. Perhaps he was right. As I turned for the kitchen, a thought prompted me to ask him for a clarification.

"When I asked whether or not I was permitted to have compassion on another human being who has been injured as that man has, you said there were two cases for which showing mercy would be inappropriate. The first was that my compassion might be used against me. I believe I understand what you meant. But you never told me the second case in which I might not be permitted to have compassion on that man. Please tell me what that might be."

Looking directly into my eyes, he replied with a clear tone, "The other situation would be if that one is not human."

I remained silent.

He continued.

"Please, you do not know what has taken place here this evening. For your own welfare and for what is facing all of us in the next few days, get your rest."

CHAPTER 3

WRESTLING

Sleep and insomnia waged a bitterly fought war that Thursday night, though the outcome was inevitable. Physical forces campaigned for sleep. Weariness from the Wednesday night drive merged with the exhaustion from the lengthy hike. Normally this duo would have been enough for ordinary opponents on average days. The hard floor of the loft and the thin bedding from my sleeping bag only served to point out where the aches originated. Leg muscles cramped when not sleeping supine. The upper back at the point of the blades and especially the neck and shoulder muscles felt aflame, particularly where the weight of the pack straps had pressed against me. No comfortable position for sleeping could be assumed. Ordinarily such aches and pains would bring on sleep. Not tonight, for this was the night of trials.

The mental and the emotional marshaled their soldiers and were more than sufficient to drive away sleep. Sympathy for the injured man was always at the surface of consciousness. Would he die before morning? Should he be protected? There was anxiety about the intercessor. Who was he? Why did he never refer to himself other than *this one*? Why did he speak of the injured man as *that one*? What dangers would be faced in the upcoming days? Fear for the woman and the boy continuously meant considering scenarios for their protection and escape. It troubled me that the only exit from the loft was the makeshift ladder. My mind exchanged and intermingled thoughts, shifting from the serious to the silly. I knew the stovepipe was not hot but several times during the night I checked to make certain the boy had not rolled against it. While such inspections relieved my mind, they also kept me awake. When one thought was driven away, another quickly took its place. What did the intercessor mean by those last words? Was the injured man human or not? For that matter, was the intercessor human? How do I compete with or escape from spiritual beings? I contrasted and compared the attributes of the good angels and the fallen angels. Could there be other non-human creatures? What were they like? Could they incarnate themselves, or at least give such an appearance?

I attempted to pray, telling God of my situation and asking for His help. Such endeavors quickly degenerated from pleading, to vowing, to bargaining and finally, convinced I was the one who must act, to the endless loops of certain story lines. I attempted to include God, but wasn't certain what that meant in the various scenes before me. Knowing His will and making application of it to the God-pleasing scenario were different things, especially when I wasn't certain of much in recent hours. Ultimately, I placed God in a secondary role as several options were selected for further thought and others were rejected. Mostly I asked myself questions. Was this inability to keep God in the forefront and on my side part of the danger awaiting me? Or, in my supplications to God, was I praying to the injured one below? Was he God? Or was the intercessor God?

Time slowed to a crawl as each second ticked in my mind. How long would it be before the dawning of a new day arrived? I concentrated on where the sun would rise relative to the shelter. The general direction of the trail was northeast. My best estimate was that the sun would curl around the mountain for a while before its rays pierced through the sparse evergreens to the east. While that might mean as late as 8:00am, I consoled myself with the hope that the first light of dawn might arrive as much as two hours earlier, perhaps more. Several times I imagined a faint cast of color declaring the advent of the sun. More than likely it was what I desired. After what seemed hours of seeing this mirage, I shut my eyes.

Rather than bringing on sleep, closing my eyes sharpened the sense of hearing. Throughout the night my ears picked up sounds from below, a voice speaking in hushed whispers, a rhythmic murmur uttered over and over. While I heard the murmurs, I could not determine the substance or the source. Other than the intoning voice, no sounds of movement came from the stalls. It occurred to me that earlier in the evening the injured man could be heard coughing. Now, whenever *now* was, I heard no sounds. I longed for a cough or a wheeze or even a moan to reassure me that he lived. But nothing sounded forth from the darkness except the hypnotic, slow-pulsing tone that lasted for eternal hours. Then unsettling and disquieting silence followed for a shorter time. The murmuring voice returned. It was maddening to be able to hear the voice but not comprehend the words.

Not only is it the coldest just before dawn, it is also the quietest. Neither those intoning whispers nor the gripping groans came from the stable stall. Snoring from the woman or the boy would have been welcome, a simple assurance that I was not the only one left in the universe with the wounded man. The cold forced the woman to curl into the fetal position in her sleeping bag. The mountain winds had been no more than a breeze the previous day and now the night passed in silence. I would have welcomed the sounds of contracting metal from the stove and its pipe. Though quiet, the pre-dawn night remained less than peaceful.

In that stillness, I understood a new dimension to hell. Certainly a portion of the awful condition is the continual burning without consumption. The tormented pain is physical, mental, emotional, spiritual and soulful. There is complete isolation from God, from His creation and from anyone else. Indeed, hell is total privation. But there is even more, or rather, there is even less. In the silence of that early morning darkness I contemplated another of hell's attributes: the total absence of sound. The mouth would be opened to wail, or to howl, or to cry out for relief and there would be no sound waves. There would not be an echo. Like a scream released into a vacuum, the sound could not reach the ear of the crier. Except for the self-conscious, mental awareness within, there could be no communication and no affirmation of the pain, no confirmation of existence. There was only the self and those yawning, silent screams of the self-tormented soul.

Mercifully, sleep came.

I awakened with a start, as if having missed something. To have remained awake so long during the night vigil only to miss the long-awaited advent of first light produced momentary pangs of regret and guilt. I recalled the hymn, "Watchman, Tell Us of the Night." But I, the unfaithful watchman, had fallen asleep at my post.

Practical thoughts quickly supplanted the awful, gnawing ones. A morning assessment of the situation caused me to chastise myself for the dominant pessimism of the night now passed. The morning light of another day preceded new hope. Along with it came with the feeling that I could accomplish something in the daylight.

As a penitent, I determined to rise, feeling justified that such resolution had some sort of divine approval. The feeling was similar to what I experienced as a little boy at nap time. Naps were unpleasant events, one reason being the unspoken rule that required staying in bed until sleep had been accomplished. To get up without having taken a nap met with mother's disapproval. Once sleep had come, no matter how short a time it might have been, getting up was justified. At those times the conscience did not accuse, but rather excused. Mother would be happy. Such silly, childlike thoughts, and yet even at this age, they remain in my mind and surface on occasion. Will such thoughts surface after I have climbed onto my deathbed?

Getting down from the loft required care. I did not want to disturb the boy and his mother. Though my aching feet protested the coming vertical position, I slipped into my boots. The boards creaked as I stiffly twisted from the sleeping bag and made my way to the ladder. Negotiating the ladder required the use of shoulder muscles still sore from the heavy pack straps and yesterday's hike.

From the loft I could not see my intercessor. The bare feet of the injured man extended beyond the stall, testifying at least to a corporeal presence. I scanned the kitchen area to ensure the absence of the intercessor. This being confirmed, I resolved to know the condition of the injured man. As I approached the stall, I became increasingly apprehensive and it occurred to me that my growing anxiety came not from concern about his physical condition, but from fear that he may have sufficiently recovered and might now be waiting to snare me. He would still be injured. The other one would not. Of course, the intercessor's declaration of the other possibility might be true.

I approached the front corner of the open room from the opposite side and peered around the edge of the stall. I relaxed. The pitiful man was in no position or condition to attack. The intercessor had cinched the injured man's hands together with a nylon rope. The other end of the rope was tethered to one of the boards above his head. The bound man, seated unnaturally on and slung uncomfortably to the side, gained support for his upper body by leaning against the rope. The circulation in his hands appeared cut off by the taut binding while his swollen hands cinched the tie even more. With his head hung low and chin resting on his chest, his face remained hidden. His brown, slightly curly hair was matted with dried sweat and blood.

He sensed my presence and slowly raised his head to look at me. A mixture of sweat, spittle and blood had dried in his beard. The blood appeared to have come from wounds on his forehead with their dried streambeds revealing an earlier flow down the contour of his face. During the night, his pain produced the white, frothy foam that issued from his mouth and dried in its corners. The side of his face, both above and below his right eye, was bruised and swollen. His dark eyes focused on me and then pierced me to my inmost being. He struggled in his attempt to

39

speak. Slowly his quivering lips parted. From deep within came his first words to me, "I thirst."

Though quietly spoken, the words reverberated and caused a momentary paralysis. I remained motionless and in a stupor. How long had I stood and gazed into the empty space between us? I seemed to experience an eternity in those few seconds. Only his voice brought me back to my senses and to his repeated request, "Water."

After retrieving a cup from the kitchen, I walked to the creek. Deep breaths of the clear mountain air filled my chest and continued to clear the cobwebs of the night. Breathing any more deeply would permit the sharp air to singe my tender lungs. The dawn light caused me to squint. The icy water in the stream would provide a refreshing drink to subdue the stagnant taste of night and satisfy my thirst. The man inside, if indeed he was a man, would have the second cup of the morning. Bending to the creek side stretched my sore leg muscles and my knee joints, in turn, registered audible, popping replies.

As I raised the cup to my mouth and drew in the first long, cool sip, my eyes focused on a tent located at the tree line. The domed, canvas tent, no more than fifty feet from the creek, must have been pitched during the night. I wondered how, during those long hours of the night, I had not heard any of the sounds of camp being set up, including the pounding of tent pegs. Five or six feet in front of the zippered tent entrance a morning fire crackled. Several large rocks hid the flames from view. The smoke, ascending and leveling off in the still air, had not yet filled the hollow formed by the small gully and the surrounding trees. A man stabilized a coffeepot above the flames. After moving to the side for a seat on a boulder, he warmed his hands by rubbing them together and turning his palms to the fire.

Having drained the cup, I wiped my mouth on my flannel shirtsleeve. I had no reason to discontinue a visual inspection of his camp, no reason except the thirsting man in the stable. It became evident that since my first drink absorbed into the system so well, the man inside would have to be satisfied with the third cup of the day. At the moment between cups I watched the camper turn his head in my direction and wave his greeting. Relieved to discover the man was not the intercessor, I continued my inspection of the squatter. I estimated him to be an older man, perhaps in his late 50s or early 60s, and considered him to be no threat to my family or me. A red plaid cap covered most of his gray hair. His thick, buckskin coat was unbuttoned and open as he sat before his fire.

After having his greeting acknowledged, he motioned me to come to his camp. The smell of the burning wood, made keen to the nostrils and sharpened by the clear mountain air in my chest, compelled me to move in his direction. I do confess it was more than an attempt at politeness that directed me to the edge of his campsite. His presence invited me and his campsite beckoned me. Having neither fear nor a desire to stay away, I drew near.

"Sit down."

His first words, spoken with slight terseness, suggested more of a command than an invitation. I hesitated, aware of suspicion caused by the events of the previous night, as well as my natural reluctance to be directed by anyone, especially another stranger.

"Some of the heat from the fire warms me. Some goes to the rocks and ground, some to the coffeepot. Still there is enough heat left for warming on this cool morning. Fire is beneficial, but it does you no good if you remain distant. To receive the blessing called heat, you not only need to acknowledge the existence of the fire and its consequent benefit, but also to be drawn to it."

My reply came as I sat down, "Thanks. Sorry, I guess I am still a bit slow this morning."

The fire drew my hands closer as I alternated rubbing them together and exposing the palms to the heat of the flames. As they absorbed the heat, my back felt cold. I smiled. My grandfather stated that men naturally stood before a fire facing away from it warming their backsides as well as the palms of their hands.

Women were different. They stood facing the fire as they absorbed the heat. The heat from the fire also warmed the palms of their hands.

"You had a disturbing night," he responded.

He appeared to present a declaration rather than a surface inquiry. What a curious man the stranger was. Normally a person would not use *disturbing* in this situation, opting for the more common *restless* or *sleepless*. These words dealt more with the physical. *Disturbing* is deeper, going to the mental or spiritual or emotional. Was he aware of the anxieties experienced during the night and the events of the confrontation in the early evening?

"Do I look that bad this morning?"

"You had a disturbing night," he repeated.

He said it with the same emphasis as before. Moments passed and I felt an increasing need to say something. Mentally I vowed to remain distant, seeking to reply with a tone that could be understood as both answer or question, "Really."

Without moving his eyes from the fire he responded quickly and without commitment, "As you say."

My frustration rose and the desire to maintain a battle of wits and words fell. It was morning. Muscles mocked; back gripped. Cobwebs still cluttered the brain. My mind wanted to remain dulled and not taxed for awhile. To change both the direction and the element of mystery in our conversation, I spoke.

"Look, I'm really not much good at conversation in the morning. Your fire feels good and my bones need to soak up some of its heat. I appreciate the invitation to your campfire. By the way, what is your name?"

"Here in the woods, among the clans of the grandchildren of Noah who live on the mountain, Gabby would be my name."

Two reactions rose from within me. First, his curious use of phrases kept me wondering. Obviously he did not consider himself to be one of the natives, as if there were any of those men left who roamed these mountains so long ago. But, how much of an outsider was he? He might be an illegal alien, perhaps an alien to more than this mountainous terrain and native land. He seemed a foreigner who learned English but used it in an odd manner; odd at least, from my point of view.

The second reaction was one of anger. This Gabby was not a polite man. Out of common courtesy I had asked him his name. He told me and, simply on the basis of good manners, he was expected to ask my name in return. Could there possibly be a culture or a society where the asking of a name would not be acceptable, especially when the other person's name had been given? I thought not and resolved to end the conversation.

"I better be on my way."

"You are angry."

"Angry? No. Perturbed? Yes."

"I am listening."

"Look, this is your camp and I am an invited guest. In order to be friendly, I asked you what your name was."

"No, you asked me what my name is."

This was too much of a hassle. This man was playing word games with me and I was not in a playful mood. "Never mind. I should go."

"No, you should stay." His temperament never changed and that tended to be a calming influence. Still I was frustrated and puzzled.

"Why? Tell me why I should stay?"

"The coffee is ready to drink. The cool water you drank from the stream refreshed you. The hot coffee from my pot will warm you."

I hesitated.

Gabby continued, "The coffee pot contains the promise and the promise within it is quite real. However, the hot coffee is of no benefit to you when it remains in the pot. Does it not now work within you a desire to receive the promise and its accompanying benefits?"

"Whatever."

"No, not whatever, not ever whatever. Whatever is a denial of the revealed truth with a Laodicean response. Whatever is the last and worst course of the four. Whatever is the tepid brewing of knowledge decomposing into ignorance along with enlightenment that is degenerating into nonchalance."

I was tempted, but remained silent. Throughout his reply, he had remained calm. He knew the response I kept within but said nothing. Without a break in his demeanor, he held the pot in the direction of my cup, indicating it was still available. I placed my cup near the spout and he poured. Steam rose from the hot coffee. The palms of my hands wrapped around the cup and my nostrils inhaled the vapors. He was right about the coffee; it warmed me. Seeking to put the best construction on his initial words while not attempting to translate his recent ones, I tried again.

"From what you say, you are not from this area. Here, when someone tells another person his name, that other person is expected to return the courtesy by asking him his name. So, why don't you ask me what my name is?"

"I already know who you are, you holy one of God."

His blue eyes focused on my brown eyes. They penetrated my soul. In that moment I sensed that he not only knew my name but much more. He had spoken the words quietly and without emotion. But what was this *holy one of God* business?

As I thought, he continued, "You asked me a question and I answered it. I asked you no question. Therefore, no answer from you was called for."

"What? What are you talking about?"

"You asked me what my name is. I answered you and asked you no question in return. As a result, any answer from you would be uncalled for."

"And will you answer any question that I ask you?"

"I am here to help you answer your own questions. However, in doing so, I do not consider foolish questions."

Slurping the coffee so that it cooled before spraying onto the roof of my mouth, I momentarily pondered what Gabby might consider a foolish question. Deciding not to pursue such a line, another thought came to mind. A smile formed within and I continued our conversation.

"Gabby, what question should I ask you?"

Without reflection, he replied immediately, "You should ask me if you ought to leave now."

While his response probably should have made me angry it rather pleased me. Perhaps I was getting to him. If so, now would not be a good time to leave. I resolved to delay my departure for awhile. Though he still made me uneasy and on the edge of anger, there was something that attracted me to remain at his campfire and in his company. There had been no notice of the passage of time during our conversation. In fact, there were noticeable gaps of time between several responses. For me, it was time to think things over. For him? He appeared to use the time to clarify his thoughts, formulate his queries and intensify his question, as well as to add timid hesitation before speaking.

At that moment it occurred to me that he had no cup and drank no coffee. Contrary to my usual manner of extended thought before speaking, I blurted out, "Gabby, why aren't you drinking any of your coffee?"

In a matter of fact tone, he replied, "I prepared the coffee for you, not for me."

This was all quite puzzling. Not really knowing what to say, I asked, "Would you like to use my cup to drink from?"

"There is no more coffee in the pot. The cup you drank was the one prepared for you. I will not drink of your cup. It was for you and you will drink it to the dregs."

"But I have already finished the coffee. You make it sound like there is more coffee. You said that there was no more in the pot. Are you speaking of something else?"

"That is not the right question to ask."

"Gabby, let me get this straight. You had a fire going before I came over here. You fixed one cup of coffee and that one cup was just for me. How did you know that I would come to your camp, or for that matter, that I would even accept your coffee once I got here?"

"You have not asked me the question that you should have asked."

"What do you mean?"

"You said earlier, 'Gabby, what question should I ask you?', and I replied, 'You should ask me if you ought to leave now.'"

"Why should I ask you that question?"

"Because it is time for you to go."

I noticed the fire was nothing more than burning coals and that the sun was halfway to its zenith.

"Why should I go? Is it because the coffee is gone, or that you tire of my words? Or, is it because the heat from the burning fire has been replaced by the rising sun?"

"Risen indeed; but these are not the reasons you should go."

A thought raced across my mind and an immediate request came out of my mouth, "Gabby, let me see the palms of your hands."

As he extended his hands, his arms were exposed from the sleeves of his coat halfway to his elbows. No marks were on his arms above the wrists. This was confirming, not surprising. There should not have been any marks on his lower arms. My anticipation heightened as he began to turn them so that I could see his palms. They were still hidden by the fists that he made. My heartbeat increased as the adrenaline flowed in hopeful expectation. Slowly he uncurled his fingers and thumbs, revealing clean, unwounded, unblemished, unscarred palms. At this sobering revelation my eyes rose to meet his. Once again his eyes forced me back and within myself. Because he mesmerized me, I feared him.

Who was this man standing in front of me? Minutes went by. Finally I managed to speak.

"Why is it time for me to go?"

"Because of the cup that awaits you."

Suddenly I remembered the injured man in the stable and his simple, basic request. I scrambled to my feet, "Oh, the cup of water for him!"

Gabby replied, "No, not that cup. Your cup."

As I hurried to get a cupful of creek water to the injured man, I did not hear Gabby's reply.

CHAPTER 4

SATISFYING THE THIRSTY ONE

Nearly three hours passed since my promise to the thirsty man. As I rinsed and filled the cup with creek water, I considered the possibility that he might be dead. Having spent hours in conversation with Gabby, I sought to make up seconds by running with the full cup. It was an awkward run with feet and legs moving as quickly as possible and the upper body and arms held straight and stiff in my attempt to glide without spilling the water.

The man remained supported by ropes, his head now slumped and facing the ground. His chin had shifted to his left side and perched on his shoulder. His eyes and lips were closed. I lowered the cup to his mouth and gently positioned its edge between his lips. Tipping to let water touch his parched mouth, I noticed his eyebrows lift. He was like an infant instinctively turning to the breast. The man eagerly sought more water and I wondered how far the liquid reached before it absorbed into his system. No doubt the first sip never left his mouth. As he drank he winced, indicating even the slightest movement caused him pain. The barbs causing such grimaces might have originated from hands, head, arms, back, ribs, neck or ears. At that moment I resolved to untie the man.

Direct light seeped into the shelter through cracks in the south side of the loft area and partially lighted the stalls. Long rays highlighted the dirt floor. There was no movement in the loft and no noise from the kitchen. The woman and the boy were probably still asleep, though from my kneeling position I could not see their sleeping bags.

The man finished drinking the water with a few spasmodic coughs. These fits caused wrenching pain. Still the need for water was greater than the resultant pain caused by receiving it. I placed the cup on the edge of the feeding trough. I quickly untied the rope and gently lowered his arms. As I did so, the man shrieked. He would have slumped to the side had I not kept some pressure on the rope. My knee served as a support for his weight when the rope loosened. This position permitted me to remove my coat. I threw it in the corner and shifted my arms in order to lower him a foot or two. Half-reclining and half-propped by the two walls in the corner, the man seemed as comfortable as circumstance allowed.

His eyes had not opened and I chastised myself for not having returned to him sooner. How long would it have taken me to get a cup of cold water to him? I did not understand what kept me from my errand of mercy. I was ashamed of myself and astounded at my thoughtlessness. Gabby had delayed me and kept me from doing this thing I promised. That old man had known this thirsty man was hurting. He detained me for hours. Then, he had reproved me for withholding a cup of cold water from the thirsty one.

The small rope dug deeply into the man's wrists. The white flesh on one side of the tightly knotted rope was offset by dark, compacted flesh on the other side. The natural swelling increased and intensified the pain. Release of the ropes did not immediately remedy the situation. The channels remained in place and the gross contrast between the lighter, bloodless tissue and the puffed-up, blood-bound, tight mass of flesh was sickening to behold. The bindings had broken blood vessels and caused him to bleed both internally and externally.

I took the cup when he had sipped, gave thanks that he had been able to drink it and decided to go to the creek for more water. With my lips pursed in indignation I looked at Gabby's camp. He was not in sight. All the better for him.

50

Back with the victim, I poured a little water over the back of one of his hands and gently massaged it for more circulation. Some of the dirt and sweat came off, revealing a large, round scar. Slowly I turned his hand over. In the palm of his hand was another scar or rather, the other side of the same scar. My immediate reaction was to drop his hand and run. The thought of inducing further pain prevented me from doing so. I released his hand after letting it rest against his thigh. The same discovery was made as I took his other hand and began cleaning it. After carefully placing this hand in a comfortable position, I surveyed his face. He opened his weary eyes and looked at me.

Barely opening his lips, he said, "Thank you."

"You're welcome .... sir."

He braced against the ground to find a more comfortable position. Wincing as he moved, the thirsty man revealed that his injuries were more than what could be ascertained from the surface. Though tempted to ask the question that is no question, but rather, a statement of wondering hope, I asked instead, "Are you okay?" The cool water quickened him, but my simple presence seemed to be appreciated as much. Supposing he had a fever, I poured the last tablespoons of water over his head. The rivulet trickled down his forehead, between his eyes and along the side of his nose. The blood from the wounds on the crown of his head had taken the same course. He was a pitiful looking human being. Contrary to common sense, logic and reason, the intercessor was right. The man before me was not mere man. I vacillated. Hadn't I, just a few minutes earlier, anticipated the same with Gabby? Maybe, because I wanted it to be, I allowed free course to my imagination.

During the wanderings of my mind, his eyes never left me. A gradual change transformed his face from a teeth-clenching grimace to a Mona Lisa smile. Self-satisfied that I had provided a cup of cold water and pleased that such an offering had accomplished some good, I asked, "What more can I do?"

"Nothing. Unless ... unless you want ... to do something."

He perceived my glance toward the silent loft, and continuing in a recovering manner, he panted out, "They're gone ... they went ... for ... a hike. I heard ... them ... say so."

How could they possibly walk past this injured man and not notice him? Why hadn't they waited for me? Could they not have stayed with this injured man for even one hour? Wait. How could I have missed seeing the woman and the boy leaving the stable when I was at Gabby's camp? Is it possible they hadn't seen me sitting at the fire, or heard us talking, or smelled the smoke? Since the situation lacked common sense and defied logic, I was bewildered. I turned my attention to the injured man once more.

"What is your name?"

"I am ... yes, I am ... I am ... known by many names."

He shifted his position once again, obviously intent on speaking to me and focusing his attention on me. He must have had injured ribs. I admired his determination and courage.

"Call me whatever you ... yes indeed, ... whatever you feel ... whatever you need me to be."

A nervous snicker came forth from me and he responded.

"Why do you laugh?"

"I didn't laugh."

"Alright, ... you didn't laugh."

"Sorry, I guess I did laugh. But I was just expressing my confusion about this whole situation. The woman and the boy left without seeing either of us. That doesn't make sense. Also, it seems I am having a problem with names this morning. You see, while I could use some answers to a number of questions, all I end up with is multiple choice. You ask me what I need? Right now, I'm not certain of the answer to your question. Since late yesterday, my thoughts haven't made much sense. Perhaps things will improve. Who are you?"

"I am ... yes, I am ... I am ... whoever you need me to be."

My frustration was obvious and after a few moments he continued.

"Look, friend ... I have always been ... whoever you needed me to be. Right now, you feel you need ... someone to listen to you. ... So, for right now, call me Confessor."

His voice had a calming effect. There was no hint of threat, only the expression of a sincere desire to help. Showing genuine concern, he leaned forward. Every word I spoke interested him. He set his pain aside and focused his undivided attention on me.

"Confessor? But isn't a confessor someone who hears the sins of another."

"Yes indeed, that is a part of the office, and a rather insignificant part. But if you pardon my saying so, sins are rather relative. Who can know his secret faults, if indeed, they are faults? Call it back-sliding. It sounds much more negotiable. Trust me, my interest with you is neither one of exposing your sins nor of condemning you."

Confessor carefully rubbed his hands together as he continued with firm conviction.

"Besides, we both know that these things are relatively unimportant. Why bring up what has been determined to be unfashionable? We need not speak of such unpleasantness again. In these times there is a more important part of a confessor's privilege, to listen to what someone believes. Of course, the emphasis is on the *listen* and not on the *what*. However, knowledge of and assent to an individual's *what* is both helpful and most necessary."

He was speaking smoothly now and without hesitation.

"You have been more than a friend to me, showing sympathy and pity while I made my bed here in this stable. When I was hurting and in need, you helped me. While I was imprisoned here you visited me. You helped me rest my head against this manger. Truly, you have done it unto me. My dear friend and my beloved brother, right now, in this state and condition I am not able to repay you for your pity, your kind mercy and your tenderhearted care. However, I can begin. While you must wait for your full reward, the least I am able to do is listen."

Both what he said and how he spoke calmed me.

He continued, "Please, my friend, tell me what you desire. Speak to me and tell me what you believe."

"What I believe? That is not the foremost in my mind right now. I would rather speak of other things."

"As you wish. We will hear what you believe a little later. Please, tell me what you will. I desire to affirm you."

"Well, if you are Confessor, I am confused and more than a little apprehensive. Last night a man walked in my direction. He followed the trail along the creek. With intense focus I watched him until that instant you suddenly appeared from nowhere and confronted me. Your appearance shocked me. It is a wonder my heart didn't burst from the intense fright I experienced. That is my first confession."

His lungs filled with an extra amount of air, though not in an attempt to control anger but as if seeking to calm me.

"Kind sir, may I present to you the possibility that a particular fear caused by a sudden warning might be good because it averted a more serious danger?"

I asked, "What do you mean?"

"Well, consider a hiker on this mountain. He is walking a mile below a dangerous snowfield. Suddenly he hears a rumble above him. The snow has broken loose and an avalanche begins cascading down the mountainside. The loud sound causes an instantaneous, awful fright. The terrified hiker has only a few golden seconds to get out of the pathway of the juggernaut. Because the sound came first and warned of imminent danger, the hiker had the possibility of escape. If he did get out of the way, it was because he was warned and the warning gave him sufficient time. He should be most thankful for the sound that warned, even though it frightened him terribly."

I asked, "Thankful to whom?"

"One moment please. You will be able to answer your own question."

I muttered something and indicated that he ought to continue.

"Now think of the hiker who is on this mountain during a sudden electrical storm. Say that lightning strikes a tree one mile away. A second later the air cracks with the sound. The hiker looks at the flash of light in amazement but the light does not evoke a reaction other than perhaps an *ohhh* or an *ahhh*. However, when the thunderclap crashes in, the hiker ducks for cover. What for? Why? The hiker will not be hurt by the sound that comes second. It is the lightning, which strikes first and without warning, that can kill the hiker. Last night, when I jumped in front of you, I was not the thunderclap sound following the killer lightning; rather, I was the wonderful, fearful, life-saving rumble from the on-coming avalanche. One sound brings a useless fear; the other sound brings a blessed fear. Now, what was your last question?"

"My last question? Oh yes. Thankful to whom?"

"Should I answer it or have you answered it yourself?"

"I understand, but I need time to think."

"That is a luxury I am afraid neither one of us has. The clock has been ticking away the golden seconds since my intervention."

"Don't you mean the clock had been ticking away?"

He answered, "If that were only the situation."

"You don't know?"

"That is for you to decide."

"What am I supposed to decide?"

"Whatever."

"Whatever?"

"Yes, whatever is what you are to decide. Whatever you decide will determine your future, your escape. It always has. It always will."

"My escape?"

"The matter of your escape remains the only unknown."

I asked in an abbreviated question, "Escape from?"

"Yes, but also escape to."

"What are you talking about, Confessor? How many escapes are there?"

"Only two. You escape from one and to the other, or you escape from the other and to the one."

"Earlier, a man told me there are four courses. So, are there two courses or four?"

He replied slowly and softly, "That is for you to say. For the next few days you ought to ponder these matters."

For several minutes the consequences of his analogy, the implications of his tense, the indifference of his whatever and the matter of the escapes were analyzed. Uncertainty remained the bottom line.

"Confessor, do you realize that you should be called my intercessor?"

"As you will. If that fulfills your need, please make it so. If it is your wish, then I am Intercessor."

"And yet, that is just what he told me he was. He rescued me from you. One of you is not telling me the truth. Perhaps it is best for me to listen."

"What is it that you want to hear? Indeed, will you trust what I say to be truth?"

"Don't you mean *the* truth?"

"Whichever. Please, my friend, I do not feel that you necessarily accept what you hear from me. Of course, that is one of the marks of someone quite wise."

While these spoken words were obviously flattering and intended to be winsome, the tone and manner in which they were vocalized, accomplished his purpose subconsciously within me. Perceiving that my hesitation was not from the rejection, but rather, from the apparent acceptance of his words, he continued.

"Wisdom knows when to be silent, my friend. Discernment is conceived in the heart of the man who is rightly cautious. Flattery finds no place to rest when the man to whom the words refer is worthy of them. They are not flattery, but mere statements of fact concerning the man."

I became mesmerized by what he said and by how he spoke. His estimation awakened pride and fed self-confidence as I absorbed his words. However, having heard his words, I was not able to repeat them at that time. Even my recitation of this account is not verbatim. Rather, it is a weak recollection of the content. His words, phrases and sentences were inhaled into my being and disappeared. Startled from stupor and back to reality, I could only recall the specific last words he spoke and responded with an awkward comment.

"... concerning the man? What about a woman?"

Confessor, even Intercessor, was pleased and leaned forward with anticipation.

"Ahh, very good. We are progressing. If inclusiveness is what you feel you need, I will gladly accommodate. Consider it done. You are not only perceptive, but you bear the mark of an open-minded, tolerant person. Now you are beginning to let me know what you believe. Continue, please."

"Why is it so important that I tell you what I believe?"

"My friend, you are not letting me be Confessor. Telling me what you believe is important to me. Right now, it is not your desire to speak of such matters. Perhaps you would prefer me to be Counselor. That is what you feel you need right now. I sense it. Please, call me, Paraclete. So, what sort of counsel do you need?"

He shifted his weight from one side to the other, doing so without apparent discomfort. I sat against the side of the open doorway with my back to the outside. The sun was warm and soothed the night aches.

"I don't know what counsel to ask from you."

"Well, what weighs on your heart right now? Certainly there are some concerns that you have. Pick the one that comes to mind first and share it with me. Tell me of your greatest desire at this moment."

"Alright, Mr. Paraclete, whatever that means, I am concerned about my safety as well as the safety of the boy and the woman."

"Good, but let's focus on you first. There might be time later to address the others. And by the way, paraclete means *comforter* or *counselor*. A paraclete is one called to be at the side of another. But please, my friend, please continue."

"Okay, okay. Advise me, Mr. Counselor."

He remained silent and waited.

"Look, when you say 'there might be time', a red flag goes up. This weekend, is the threat to me of a physical or spiritual nature?"

"That is a reasonable question. But, are you so sure that you can separate them? In other words, isn't there a dimension to both in every event in life? What you should be concerned with is the target of the attack, not the source. We will deal with the source at another time. For now, concentrate on where you feel threatened. In the hours since twilight yesterday evening, which have you feared for, your body or your soul?"

"To be honest, my first reaction was for my life, and for the physical safety of the woman and the boy."

"Fine. Has any bodily harm come to you?"

"No," I admitted and added quickly, "though the stress has physical consequences."

Listening to his questions and responding to them was becoming easier. He was leading me through a helpful, objective evaluation of the events. It was good to have a perspective of the events from someone else's point of view.

"And why is that? What, or who, has come between you and any physical harm?"

"You are the only one who has been injured. You came between the intercessor and me, or rather I should say, between the man who unmercifully attacked you and me. Truly, I perceive that you are the intercessor. Willingly and without having to be asked, you took upon yourself the brutality intended for me."

"Exactly. The only one whom you should fear is the one who is capable of harming you physically."

"But I do have other fears."

"They are secondary."

"But Confessor, I have suffered mental, emotional and psychological pain since the attack took place. I do not wish to minimize the hurt that you have endured, but these other pains exist as well. Worry, uncertainty and anxiety are pains of the mind, aches of the heart and longings of the soul. Maybe I am even experiencing some grief, responsibility and regret for what you are going through."

From his demeanor I could tell he was pleased.

"Today you understand that you are not able to separate the physical from the spiritual. This is good. You have progressed. You were the target of physical pain. Suddenly you discover that you were also the target of spiritual pain. So, you are ready. Now move from the targets to the sources. You have correctly indicated that the source of the intended physical wounds was the attacker. That was from outside yourself and could be prevented only by my absorbing it in your stead. Think, my friend. Where have your spiritual, mental and emotional pains come from?"

This was becoming easy. Everything took on a needed and much appreciated clarity.

"Those pains came from within me, from my own mind as I sorted through all of the possibilities and ran the various scenarios to their logical conclusions. The assaults upon my soul originated from fortresses within me. I would seem to be my own worst enemy."

"True, but you can be your own best friend. The power to do so is within you."

"Yes, but must I rely only on myself? Are you not able to help me?"

"I am able. Know this, my friend, the power is within and it is the power and determination and ability to tolerate and adapt. Listen to your own natural feelings. In fact, even if the result is a feeling of contrition and remorse, you must have the inner strength and courage to ignore the very fact that I took your place last night. Repression does you no good. Cast all your cares away. The only one you have to fear is the one who can destroy both body and soul, and that one, is you."

Talking with him became pleasurable and hypnotic. He accompanied me along the way and as we came to obstacles, he guided me past them. There was an inner yearning to trust him and the yielding to the call was most pleasant. He focused on me, my life, my troubles, my felt needs, my beliefs. He understood me.

"Counselor, why are you so interested in hearing what I believe? The topic is very important to you."

"Yes it is. Do you want me to be Confessor now?"

"No, not really. But tell me this, why does it matter to you what I believe?"

His face resembled an old grandfather patiently enduring the questions of children. He was pensive and sensed the need for me to reflect on what I had asked. Finally he began his answer.

"Back up and think a moment. You do not understand the issue. *What* you believe is not important to me and should not be to anyone else. *That* you believe is crucial. You must believe something. Believing something follows your choice. You must choose. Those who are condemned are those who will not make a choice. Again, the important matter is not the something that is believed, but rather, the choosing of it and the believing itself."

Coaxed by his words, I nodded my head in approval. The world was full of people of differing beliefs, but each one chose. On the other hand, I had seen the look on the faces of people who could no longer choose and who had lost all belief. With such forfeiture they lose the zest for life and with it, hope. They have abdicated any right to salvation. The Intercessor licked his lips and was looking healthier. The water must certainly have revived him. He continued.

"The betrayer committed suicide because he couldn't believe in me any more."

"The betrayer? Who is it you are talking about?"

"One very close to me, one of my disciples. But he became incapable of believing in anyone other than himself, and then he discovered that he didn't believe even in himself. He lost all hope because he had no faith. In order to have hope and life, there must be faith. The object of that faith is not important. The possession of faith is critical because it involves selection. Believing gives purpose, hope and a meaning to life that -"

Abruptly his face darkened. He cowered and quickly scooted backward and into the black shadows of the corner. Grunts of pain mingled with growls of enmity. A seething sound issued forth as when air is forcefully breathed through foamy teeth clenched in fearful anger. He melted into the darkened niche as the light was blocked at the doorway behind me. My hair bristled and my heartbeat increased. I prayed it was the woman. I longed for it to be the boy. I even hoped it might be Gabby. But I knew who it was.

CHAPTER 5

NAMES

"Do you hear me, Naive One?"

Awakening from a stupor, I discovered I was standing far above the timberline gazing at Gabby's camp below. Beyond Gabby's tent, through the woods and across the creek, I saw the shelter. No one stirred in either place as I continued to stare. While I could hear, see and think, no movement came from me. I was mesmerized to the point of paralysis. A voice spoke but it came as through a long tunnel. My eyes functioned but they were only windows taking pictures of two-dimensional landscape images. The brain received, and yet processed, no information.

"Come on. Get with it. Focus. I know you can hear me. Snap out of it."

His voice did not cause me to move. Rather, a continued gentle breeze in my face dried the surface of my eyeballs. The initial tingle gave way to a burning sensation that increased the longer I remained unblinking. My eyes registered their complaint to the brain and I willed them to close. But willing and doing are not the same. The burning became painful. Only after an extended time of resolute determination, I blinked. Doing so returned me to the brink of acting freely on my will. I kept my smarting eyes closed and pressed my palms against them. I bent over until my elbows rested on my thighs. The stinging of the eyes was healing pain as the dryness gradually departed

Simultaneously, I willed that he go away, but I knew that willing and making it happen were two different endeavors, the latter being far beyond my control. I hoped I had been dreaming, but gave up such a thought when I heard the voice again. The waterlogged, tunneled utterances of one far away, was replaced by the voice of the first intercessor who stood beside me.

"Stand up, for you will be examined. Prepare yourself as one under trial. I am going to question you and you are going to answer me."

I heard him, but the fuzziness of my mind needed attention and an answer; both required time and clarity.

"How did I get up here so far from the shelter?"

"Listen to me, Naive One. You are the one who will provide the answers."

A defiant, triune fearlessness, born of confusion, fatigue and frustration, emerged from me and I asked, "Why?"

"You will not ask the questions!"

His voice dropped an octave and increased in volume. Vibrations struck the hairs that danced on the back of my arms and neck as he thundered, "Where were you when this mountain range was formed? What part did you have in the creation of that valley? Answer me if you are able."

No response was given, nor did I intend to give him one. I waited until my mind became clear, granting precise thoughts and yielding elaborate reflections. Oddly, the old saying came to me, "Yours is not to reason why, yours is but to do or die." Rather than asking a question, a strange inkling formed and I placed a possibility before him.

"A cat that is not hungry might catch a mouse and, rather than killing it immediately, will let it go for a second or two. The mouse begins to run away, only to be pounced on. The cat is playing with the mouse and will do so until the game becomes boring. Then the cat kills the mouse with one vicious bite and walks away."

I waited, received no response and continued, "You are most capable of killing me at any moment. Are you keeping me around for sport, or do you have some other sadistic purpose?"

"Truly, I am the cat. I am the lion who must claw you deeply lest you slacken in your resolve to resist the temptations of the other one."

There was no hint of threat in his voice, only firm declaration. My determination to maintain a front against him stayed firm.

"In our conversations, you always refer to that man as the other one or as that one. You even suggested to me that he is not human. Perhaps he is; perhaps he is not. I don't really know. But if I am a prisoner to conversation with you, as indeed, it truly appears I am, then I insist you call him by name. Which of his names are you going to use?"

"He has but one name. Chameleon. It is the very nature of that one to attempt to be all things to all humans that by whatever means necessary people might come under that old serpent's lost, dismal domain. Chameleon simmers many juicy sauces to discern the personal and preferred Turkish delight. Once discovered, you are half caught in the web. Chameleon converses only for the purpose of knowing which name appeals the most to the victim. Which names did that one try out on you or suggest that you use? If I were that one, knowing you as I do now, I would attempt to have you address me as Beloved Father, Counselor or Brother. Tell me, Ignorant One, what did you call that one? Have I guessed correctly?"

What he said about the names did make sense to me. Whether Chameleon's intent and purpose were as he claimed I did not know. I would make no judgment at this time concerning intentions. Neither would I answer his question. I resolved to remain undecided, not knowing whether this was because I didn't want to give him the satisfaction of knowing he had guessed correctly, or because I wanted to keep him from knowing too much.

"And you, sir, what is your name?"

I sensed his awareness of my deflection and of my determination not to be intimidated. "Obtuse One, are you asking me what my name is or who I am?"

As I pondered the options and offered no reply, I attempted to appear aloof.

He continued, "There is no need for you to think on this. The outward form of my name is based upon the substance of my being. My name is a declaration of my essence, of my being. I am Tetra Graham."

"What is meant by your name, Tetra?"

With obvious indignation, he inhaled slowly and deeply. In a deliberate manner he raised his head in an obvious gesture of indignation and superiority. His eyes trained on mine.

"You will call me by my name. My name is Tetra Graham. Not one of your attempts to be cute, novel, informal or familiar will be tolerated. You use my name or be prepared for the consequences of dealing with me apart from what has been revealed to you. Likewise you will not title my name with mister, sir, master or comrade. Neither shall you add prefixes or suffixes to my name. You must neither take from nor add to my name. I am Tetra Graham."

"Whatever."

"Whatever! Do not ever use that word. I am what I am. I do not change. Only by my mercy are you not cast into the depths of the deepest ocean at this moment."

"Whatever you say. Anyway, my name is ..."

"Wait fool! I already know your name and its form does not follow either your essence, one of your major characteristics, your locale or what you do. You are poorly named. Do you think it an accident that I now address you as Uprooted One? Your parents named you improperly. That is a most irresponsible tradition of your culture."

"Would you kindly tell me what you are talking about, Tetra Graham?"

5

"Yes, if you need such instruction. In advanced societies, centuries before yours, people took the name of their occupation. A man who worked in the field called himself Farmer. Farming is what he did and Farmer was his name. Others took and gave names like Barber, Carter, Miller, Fuller, Wagoner, Baker, Fletcher and Carpenter. People from more advanced cultures understood that names are more than sentimental words and as a result, they were careful in the selection of a name. An individual attribute may be incorporated into a name that gives stature, depth and meaning. Listen to me, Puny One, don't you recall the names of Henry the Fowler, Simon of Cyrene, Crazy Horse, Shoeless Joe Jackson, Attila the Hun, Eric the Red, Richard the Lion-Hearted, James the Lesser, Simon the Zealot and Mary, Queen of Scots. Hearken your ear to me, Blithering Idiot. A personal characteristic may decide what one is to be named. Esau means hairy. Melody would be an appropriate name for a girl who sings well. It is entirely proper for a healthy baby boy to be named Eugene. The name means good beginning or wellborn. Sophia is the mother who uses this name for a healthy boy. These names have meanings. Sadly, people like you misuse the name Eugene by shortening it to Gene. You take away the intended meaning with personal attempts to be contemporary. Do you understand, Sniveling One?"

"You know, you really are aggravating. Perhaps I should call you -"

"Perhaps you should not."

Considering his ability to transport me from the stable to this location in an instant, I did not want to irritate him further.

I continued, "It seems to me that you take all of this name business a bit too far. Is it all that important?"

"Absolutely!"

"But you changed my name several times."

"Indeed I have. People would be wise to consider renaming themselves and others. Names should change and this is not without precedent in the history of the world. Jacob, which

66

means supplanter, was renamed Israel, which means one who wrestles with God. What was once a matter of accepted practice should be a required action in your civilization today. A woman named Irene who develops combative behavior should be renamed Enmity. An old man named Eugene who dies in his sleep should be remembered as one whose final name became Euthanasia."

The laugh within was restrained, but he detected the smirk on my face. Tetra Graham said nothing, evidently enduring my humored response by remaining silent. A thought came to mind and I decided to pursue the topic of discussion.

"Tetra Graham, your point about names is well-taken, but I am not sure about changing names. Have you changed names?"

"No, I change not. I am Tetra Graham."

"Do you have other names?"

"Yes."

"Would you tell me some of them?"

"No. They are revealed as I will."

"Something puzzles me. While you obviously favor having the name fit the person and suggest making one or more changes during the lifetime of an individual, you give absolutely no latitude to Chameleon. If you could, please explain this to me."

"If I could?"

"If you would."

"Listen to me carefully and learn. Chameleon is well-named. That one changes names, not because of personal, essential characteristics or attributes, but because that one strives to suit the felt needs of others. Chameleon's purpose is to stalk its prey, to deceive by guise, to commune with the victim, to gain confidence by appearing to be of like mind and then to possess the prey. Now think for a moment, Naive One. What is your weakness and how has it been exploited?"

I remained silent in thought.

He continued, "I'll answer for you. You have a propensity for compassion and an inclination to be the center of attention. Your society has defined love in terms of individualistic tolerance, and you, whether you acknowledge it or not, have been influenced by your culture. Therefore, Chameleon comes to you seeking a relationship with you based upon one of the names I suggested to you earlier. Chameleon's essence has never changed. Form follows function, style is based on substance. From the beginning, that one has been the same."

"I understand, but please do not take such understanding as my personal agreement or the assent of my heart."

His voice deepened, "Listen, Naive One, your personal agreement or disagreement to what I have told you does not concern me. Likewise, I could not care less about the assent of your heart. Your believing, anti-believing, trusting, not believing, mock-believing, unbelieving, make-believing or non-believing are nothing. Your choosing is without significance. Rather, the set standard is chosen for you, Burdened One."

He spoke of a subject about which Chameleon and Gabby were most emphatic. The topic began to interest me, though I did not have a position formulated. This lack of position did not necessarily put me in agreement with either Chameleon or Gabby. Likewise, I was not of a disposition to make the same confession as Tetra Graham. Though questions remained, my interest piqued.

"What do you mean? Isn't my believing of primary importance? What I believe makes all the difference in the world, doesn't it?"

"It is time to have another name change, Myopic One. You drivel along thinking you are addressing only one assertion. You are not. Your believing and what you believe are not the same. Believing is a subjective activity and of no value. What you believe is objective reality. This is the law. Your believing and the standard are different and you must be careful. You have been listening to Chameleon."

"Well ... look, Tetra ... uh, Tetra Graham, I feel and I believe. These are very important to me."

He looked at me in disgust and repugnance. In addition to the fact that Tetra Graham was at least six inches taller than I, he stood uphill from me. His height appeared to increase as he towered over me. My neck ached from straining to view his face.

He thundered, "No. Neither your feeling nor your believing nor your choosing determines the truth. The law is truth. It is the code. There is an objective standard that does not rely upon your feeling, your emoting, your willing or your believing. You have absolutely no bearing on the truth. If something is true, then it is true because of the objective fact that is outside of and beyond your petty, sappy, puny, sniveling, personal feeling or believing. Accept this as the truthful standard and code: you and your believing are insignificant and inconsequential. You are required to assent to the law, Redundant One. You have no choice. That is all."

Stung by his personal attack as well as his disregard for me, I asked, "It is obvious to me that what you have just said is what you feel and believe. I just accept it as your understanding of a truth. Are you not able to just accept mine?"

"Don't trifle with me, Burdened One. Is gravitation an absolute reality, or is it not? Answer me."

The question seemed simple. Still, I hesitated, reluctant to answer since he might bring in some supernatural or metaphysical argument to trick me. Finally, I responded, "At first glance, without thinking this out completely, yes, simple gravity appears to be an absolute."

He shook his head in disgust and continued, "Does gravity exist even if someone denies it?"

"Yes, as long as you are not playing word games with me."

"I don't play."

"Okay."

"Fine. Now tell me, where are we standing right now?"

I answered, "On the side of a mountain. There are rocks and gritty sand all around us. Scrub plants are scattered about us. What's the point?"

"Do you see a cliff here?"

"A cliff? No, there's no cliff here."

Tetra Graham continued in an increasingly mocking voice, "So you do not believe there is a cliff here? You don't feel that there is a cliff here? You just don't sense a cliff here, do you? Tell me what's on your heart about this cliff. Are you believing cliff right now?"

"There's no cliff," I replied.

"It is what you are feeling. Is it what you are believing?"

"Yes."

He continued, "So what you believe and feel determines what is true, is that correct?"

"Okay, is this a trick question?"

No word of response came from him.

"Alright, maybe over there a mile away or so there might be a steep edge in that ravine. But right here in front of me there is no cliff."

Without discernable movement on his part or mine, and with no lapse of time or consciousness, we stood at the edge of a shear cliff. The edge of the cliff suddenly appeared at my feet and Tetra Graham stood behind me. I hadn't moved anywhere by the force of another or by the exertion of my own will. I do not believe I was moved to arrive at this location. If anything, it came to me. The abyss extended down and beyond my sight, at least hundreds, perhaps thousands of feet. While questions concerning its length and location down the mountain did not concern me at this time, they would be of importance to me later. My primary attention focused on the ledge in front of me, particularly the vertigo I was experiencing. The toes of my boots hung over the edge and I screamed as I groped for the solid earth behind me. In an attempt to go down on all fours, I teetered from dizziness and nearly fell over the edge. I circled my arms around the legs of Tetra Graham and grasped tightly.

"Do not hold onto me."

I ignored his command.

In a voice laced with mockery, he queried, "What is wrong with you? You are shaking with fright. You are whimpering. I am not sure that you believe what you just told me. You said there was no cliff here because you neither believed there was nor felt there was. Now you are acting as if there was one, or, as if there were one? Which is it? Do you pose a reality, or a contrary-to-fact condition? You have a number of questions to answer. Be quick about it."

In anger I wanted to reply, "You idiot!" However, fear of Tetra Graham and my stunned recovery from the shock prevented me from responding vindictively with any verbal assault of my own.

When finally able to respond, I answered, "It changed. The cliff did not exist, and now, it is here. Certainly I believe that there is a cliff here right now. But a change has taken place."

"No. All things are as they were. There is no cliff here."

Still grasping his legs, I shouted, "Seeing is believing!"

"No," he said calmly, "it isn't, Thoughtless One. Seeing is only seeing. You may see a cliff that isn't there. Indeed, file this in your puny brain for future reference, you might even not see a cliff that really is near you. But let's not get ahead of ourselves. I, Tetra Graham, tell you this, Frightened One, if seeing is believing then you have no object to your belief. There is no cliff here."

I turned my head enough to look slightly behind me.

"It's here."

"There is no cliff here. Let me demonstrate that to you."

I gave my approval and he waited.

"Do not hold onto me. Before I am able to do what must be done, you need to let go of my legs."

I did and he immediately stepped from my semi-circled arms. As he moved to the edge I gasped. Without hesitating, he stepped over the edge and walked five or six feet into the thin air.

"Is seeing believing, or is experiencing vertigo believing? If so, what is the source of your belief? Now, please tell me if you believe in the absolute truth of gravity, or if you maintain your belief that there is a cliff here? If seeing is believing, then do you see a cliff here, or do you see me standing on the ground, or both?

71

No, don't tell me, Shivering One, ... show me. Do the deed. Fulfill the law. I am telling you that there is no crevasse, no abyss, no precipice here. There is only solid ground. That is objective truth. So, walk out here and join me. Behold the standard. Do the deed."

As I hugged the ground with one cheek against the gritty topsoil, I closed my eyes and willed both he and the crevasse to go away, willed that they disappear into thin air. But I did not believe that either would be gone if I looked. Suspended in mid-air, he waited for my answer. Opening my eyes I scanned the ground around me and saw a rock the size of my fist nearby. The light gray rock had two bright green patches of lichen on it, uncharacteristic of other rocks in the immediate vicinity. I took the rock and pitched it over the edge of the cliff in Tetra Graham's direction. An instant later I heard the sound of a sandy plop. The rock rested on the same invisible plane where Tetra Graham stood.

"Feeble One, you have only succeeded in making your predicament more dismal. Let me help you out of your dilemma. Your cowering position on the ground and choosing a substitute for the test indicate that you believe in the objective reality of the effects of gravity. You fear gravitation here even though your little test tells you that there is no cliff here. So, at this point, you want to believe in an objective gravitation, not in your personal observations and tests."

In submission I declared, "I believe in gravity."

"No! Have you not learned anything? What does it take to educate you? Listen once more and be clear about this. Whether or not you believe in gravity is not important. Have you got that?"

"Yes."

"You do not have to believe the law. You possess it. No emotional ascent to the law of gravity is needed. No heartfelt acceptance is required. No understanding is necessary. No trust. No faith. Simply own and acknowledge it in your head and abide by the law, doing the deeds that it requires. If you transgress the law, you pay the price. Otherwise, as long as you abide by the law, the benefits are yours without any belief in it. Gravitation is an objective reality without your confession of it."

I was beginning to understand even though, according to Tetra Graham, understanding was not necessary. If he was right, then there were absolute truths in the universe and these would not be found only in the physical realm. There would even be truths about God Whose benefits could be enjoyed without faith. Fulfill the requirements of the standard and you will receive your reward. The doing of the commandments brings its reward. If you obey the law of gravity and do not test it, the law will not crush you. It made sense. Could one have such blessings simply by an academic acceptance to an objective set of teachings? It seemed so. I was intrigued so I asked Tetra Graham a question.

"What is truth?"

An expression of satisfaction flowed across his face. "It has been a long time since I heard that question asked. But please, Growing One, we will speak of this later."

I had another question to ask, but if I learned anything, it was to ask my questions properly. So I began with my carefully worded query.

"According to what I have learned from you today I believe in the- No, wait. From this that you have said, the *what* is to be believed. This *what* is far more important than the fact *that* a person believes. Right?"

"*That* never matters at all. *What* is always the issue of critical importance. Possess the *what* and the *what* possesses you. Then leave it alone. Think no more on it. Accept with your head the objective reality of gravity and then go about your business. You do not have to go around saying, 'I believe in gravity, I accept the law of gravity. I obey gravity.' Forget about it and go on with the business of your life. When this occurs, the benefits are yours, whether you are speaking about gravity or time or any other absolute. When you do this, these absolutes work for you and they are always yours apart from your continued personal

73

believing or trusting or confessing it in some sort of silly creed. Then both the *that* and the *what* concern you no more."

"Tetra Graham, thank you. I have learned much from you this day, from your wise words concerning belief and names. That reminds me. I was curious about your name and what it means. Are you willing to tell me the meaning of your name?"

He replied with a short, "I am."

Nothing more was said and I certainly did not want to say, "I'm waiting" or "go ahead" for that would have given the impression he was at my service. After a few moments of careful reflection and, with a reasonable certainty that he would say nothing more, I invited, "I'm listening."

"Fool!" was the roar that came from his mouth.

The blast sent sand into my eyes, ears and hair. Tucking into a fetal position, I covered my face with my arm and shirt. I confessed to myself, "I believe that's an appropriate name."

CHAPTER 6

DARK DESCENT

After the sound like that of many waters gave way to the tranquility of a deserted place, my ears strained to detect the presence of Tetra Graham. The wind decreased from what surely had been hurricane force to mere wisps of a late afternoon mountain breeze. I dared to part my eyelids. Against the ground, my left eye could see nothing. My other eye, still screened by my shirtsleeve and arm, detected only the sky to the far right. I neither heard the booming voice from above nor saw the dark silhouette of Tetra Graham against the blue sky.

Momentarily persuaded of safety, I raised my head a few inches to scan the skewed horizon. He no longer stood in the expanse about me. Hours had passed though I did not perceive the passage of time. The sinking sun at my back cast my shadow some three to four feet beyond me. The lack of any other shadow comforted me. It provided proof that Tetra Graham was not standing behind me, though I must confess my lack of confidence concerning his absence. He might have no shadow and still be standing behind me. However, sufficiently convinced that the principles of light and optics remained valid and in effect, such thoughts requiring the suspension or violation of various laws of nature were dismissed from my mind.

In their place a revelation surfaced. Not only had Tetra Graham vanished, but also the yawning crevasse had closed or disappeared. I was no longer at the edge of the cliff. I rose to a reclining position and surveyed all 360 degrees. I saw no sign of anyone. I saw no precipice and had doubts concerning the reality of what I had seen earlier. Had it ever been there? Was the episode all a dream? An illusion? Such speculations were dashed when my eyes focused on the light gray rock with the two bright green patches on it, still at the place where I had tossed it. The earth between this stone of witness and me appeared solid. Supporting myself with one arm, the other extended a hand to determine the possibility of solid ground between the rock and me. It was all there, firm terra firma. In my mind's ear, I heard Tetra Graham's ridicule.

I turned to a seated position facing down the mountain. Leaning forward, I rested my chin on clasped hands. Less than a mile separated me from Gabby's camp and the shelter. The sun would probably set before I reached it. Anxiety led to self-chastisement for failing to take note of the location of the cliff line down the slope. While certainty existed in my mind that there was no precipice in the area, there co-existed some doubt ... enough unbelief to keep my descending route at least one hundred feet to the west.

The descent began with difficulty. Boulders, some as large as four feet in diameter, required me to do some scooting, bending and climbing down-slope. As the sun leisurely disappeared, the field of boulders gradually gave way to patches of glacial rubble. While the terrain made the walking easier, the downhill jaunt became more difficult and demanding. A walking pace quickly evolved into a stilted trot. Momentum built with the constant pull of gravity while slowing or stopping strained the legs. Thigh muscles burned with the continued exertion and unusual stress. I cursed the law.

A moment of rest provided an opportunity to behold the living portrait of a dying day. The western sky was arrayed in orange, red and purple with said colors dimming the farther my eyes went from the spot of the setting sun. When I turned to continue down, I discovered that darkness surrounded me.

76

Precious moments of travel time were lost as I waited for my eyes to dilate for the darkness ahead. Firmly resolving to avoid glances at the western sky, I also knew I would avoid any path leading near the uncertain and unseen eastern precipice.

At that moment Tetra Graham's words came to mind.

Indeed, file this in your puny brain for future reference, you might not see a cliff that is near you.

I cursed him and continued in fear.

The nearly full moon and a few bright stars dominated the evening sky. The greater of these night-lights was bright and cast helpful beams on the assumed landscape. Unable to resist the desire to discover if moon musing had the same consequences as glancing at the sunset, I peeked. Quickly I forced myself to return to my downhill observations. Eastern sky gazing was to be avoided. The light from above illuminated my path, which is where my eyes needed to remain focused. In order to return to the shelter without falling and injuring myself, I determined to abide by my own law of directing my eyes on the way. I discovered I could will this discipline but not do it. Each time my eyes wandered, I rebuked and admonished myself for the lack of self-discipline. I reminded myself that this self-imposed rule was for my own good, for my safety. Still, my eyes wandered.

The pace slowed dramatically after I crossed into the timberline. Shadows cast behind the trees necessitated careful examination of each step. An undetected hole or a hidden rock could cause a dangerous fall. A large depression ahead of me took the greatest care. Four trees to the left, the dense stand of timber straight ahead and the mound on the downhill side of the basin combined to leave the area in complete darkness. My feet discovered what must have been two outcroppings of rock at the bottom. I considered what else might be on the floor of this depression ... logs to trip me, spiked branches to poke out an eye, a jagged rock to break a leg or crack my skull. Such considerations made me probe my way with care through this depressed piece of ground. I shivered at the possibility of a creature within the darkness seeking someone to devour. An animal, a human, Tetra Graham or even Chameleon could be lurking about this sunken world. Such contemplations moved me to quicken my pace through this valley of the shadows.

After several anxious moments the mound on the far side loomed before me. A look upward revealed a promising blush of light. Scaling with both hands and feet, the short climb out of the basin began. I wanted to hurry out of that deep place for there was the constant feeling I might not escape. A final lunge from behind could snare my leg. Despite scratching and scraping the terrain as I grasped for a hold, a predator could reel me in. Such a stalker might receive a great deal of pleasure in snatching me away at the last possible instant so that, at just the time hope had been born, dread would overtake. The emotional swing from the height of expectant joy to a valley of hopelessness below served up a fine feast for one who craved and fed on quality despair. For such a one, the greatest satisfaction would not be in simply possessing the body of the prey, but in the very stalking and owning of its soul, in slaking the hunger for despair while feeding on the futility of the victim.

Cresting the mound, I found myself in the light of Gabby's campfire. His presence evoked both excitement and reverent fear. Had I not recently emerged from a frightful experience with Tetra Graham, I might not have felt this way. But the light, even though it be a dimly burning candle or a smoldering campfire, is greatly appreciated when one has been in uncertain darkness. Triggered by the aromas of Gabby's cooking I was drawn to the banquet at his campsite.

At the edge of the camp, only fifteen feet or so from the fire, I hesitated. I hoped that the spiritual challenges and physical demands encountered this day had concluded. After inhaling deeply, I exhaled and relaxed simultaneously. Gabby, though I knew he was aware of my presence, paid no attention to me. He tended a couple of sausages over the fire. Fat and juices dripped through the grill and sizzled on the coals. Something steamed in a skillet. Wisps of aroma ladened steam escaped and sent forth an inviting message. Two slices of wheat bread were toasting on a make shift rack. A small saucepan simmered at the edge of the grill.

In a manner seemingly quite ordinary, Gabby said, "The meal is quite real, but it does you no good if you remain distant."

There was neither argument nor debate from me this evening. Being drawn closer to the fire, I paused and looked to the shelter. Light could be seen, probably from the kitchen.

Gabby spoke again, "The woman and the boy have already eaten at my campsite. They returned from hiking a couple hours ago. The boy needs time with the woman. I told them you would be stopping here for supper."

"Thank you. That was kind of you to feed them."

Gabby handed me a plate, fork and knife. As I sat down he grabbed the skillet, removed the lid and slid three steamed eggs onto my plate.

"The salt is beside you." Next came sausage and toast. He continued, "The butter is there. That small jar by the pepper has blackberry preserves for your toast. Start on that while I get something for you to drink."

He used the imperative, a command. But gladly and willingly I did as directed. A thought came from the distant days of my youth. An old teacher of mine once forged the saying into my mind, "I don't have to do this, I get to do it."

A faint smile came to my face and I spoke, "Gabby, this is really something. Thank you. Your camping trip up here seems to be for the purpose of cooking our meals and feeding us."

He took the saucepan and poured hot milk into a cup. While stirring in some cocoa, he responded, "Indeed, that is one of the reasons I am here."

While I had known Gabby only a few hours and spoken with him for a matter of minutes, I recognized him as one who did not make jokes. My inner urge to chuckle never came close to emerging. He was serious to the point where humor appeared to have no place. From my brief conversations, he also did not seem one to have fits of anger or rage. After a swallow of jellied toast, I continued the conversation, "Cooking is but one of the reasons you are here? Tell me, Gabby, what's another reason you're here?"

He continued stirring the cup of hot cocoa. "To answer a few of your questions and to help you answer some of your other questions."

The clean plate in my hand was exchanged for the steaming cup. "Thank you, Gabby. Why hot cocoa instead of coffee?"

"Coffee is a morning drink that awakens. At night it keeps you awake and away from your dreams. Hot cocoa is a night drink which puts you to sleep and encourages you to have those night visions."

He was cleaning up now and I asked, "Did you eat with the woman and the boy?"

"No."

"Aren't you hungry?"

"No, I have received food."

"Gabby, you make it sound like your food is something other than what you just cooked. What did you eat?"

"My food is to do the will of the one who sent me."

I did not respond, instead opting to mull his meaning as I digested my supper. The unspoken question was, "Who are you, Gabby?" Maybe I would ask him, but not tonight. He might answer it. Gazing into the fire, I relaxed from the meal. Gabby had cleaned the cook ware and supper dishes and was putting the last clean plate away.

"Gabby, do you know Tetra Graham and Chameleon?"

"Yes."

"Who are they?"

"I will help you answer that question, but I will not answer it for you."

"What can you tell me? I am tired and the thought of attempting much thinking wearies me even further. Your food has satisfied my hunger, but now sleep is what I need."

"Before you are able to discover the answer to that question, you will need to consider what you are being asked to believe and not believe. Think on what has happened to you, on what has been said to you and on what I have just told you. Consider these things as you fall asleep this night."

I yawned. "Gabby, I'm not sure I will be able to stay awake much longer. I may have to sleep on it."

"As you wish."

"Good night, Gabby." After taking a couple steps away from the camp, I turned around and added, "Thanks for the meal and all you have done."

He replied, "I am an unworthy servant for I have only done what was my duty. Good night."

The night air was cold and my back felt it. Blowing on my fingers and rubbing my hands together warmed them. However the back, once the cold sunk in, remained that way for hours. As I approached the shelter I knew that Chameleon would be on the left side, hidden in the dark corner. I did not care.

"Hello, my good friend."

"Please, I do not want to talk. I am very tired."

Chameleon responded, "You look tired. You have been tested and are weary from the assault. You should get some rest. It will do you good. Sometimes it is best for a friend to be silent. I will say no more. Rest well."

Out of a sense of duty and responsibility, I added, "Look, is there anything that you need before I go up to sleep?"

"Do you need me to need something from you?"

Frustrated, my answer was a firm, "No."

"Then believe me, my friend, I need nothing. I am fine."

The candle in the kitchen had been extinguished and I knew the woman and the boy were already asleep. I climbed the ladder to the loft as quietly as my weary body permitted. It mattered little. The woman breathed the deep breaths of sleep. The boy slept that undisturbed slumber of the young.

With my boots finally off and set to the side, I climbed into the cool sleeping bag. Warm, sweaty feet in a cold sleeping bag tend to awaken one. There would be a few minutes to meditate on what Gabby proposed, and then a moment or two for my prayers.

"Chameleon claims that it is not the object of belief which is important but the act of believing. Choosing, not the choice, is the great virtue of humanity. Individual human opinion is what is to be stressed. Tetra Graham declares the opposite. The objective element is foundational while the subjective is immaterial. Possess the absolute truth. Hmmm. I wonder what would happen to someone if a personal belief conflicted with an absolute truth? What if a society decided to vote against an absolute truth and began to practice the decision? Could be disastrous. Of course, that would depend upon the individual circumstance and the graveness of the truth's violation. I don't know. That dilemma was faced earlier with the test of gravity and my belief in the cliff. I'm not thinking clearly. Maybe things will make more sense in the morning. ..... Hmmm. What would happen to a society if the consensus of popular opinion began to deviate from an absolute truth which is universally accepted? Like, say magnetism or electromotive force? ... Hmmm. ... What would happen if an irresistible force met an immovable object? No, I'm getting sloppy with my thought. Okay, how about this? What would happen to a nation if the consensus of popular opinion began to deviate from an absolute truth? How about deviating from several absolute truths? How many absolute truths are there? When does freedom become license? Is there such a thing as the tyranny of freedom? Is there the freedom of dogma? ... Hmmm. ... I'm not certain I am thinking clearly. I am getting sleepy. ... What causes a civilization to fall? Would it be when the people begin denying the existence of a conscience or of a god who holds people accountable? Would a greater deviation result in a more rapid destruction of society? Sodom and Gomorrah. Did they vote or did they decide by default? ... What if human laws were passed that were in conflict with laws of nature, or, if they contradicted conscience or the rule or God? ... Hmmm. What would be a good example? ... I'm so sleepy."

I did not get to my prayers before I fell asleep.

CHAPTER 7

THE DREAM GAME

"Alright, people. Find a place to sit. I have a couple things to remind you of before we go out there and play ball today."

Men, women and children gathered around the team manager and sat on benches, chairs and stools.

"Quiet down. ... Alright. As you know, this is opening day of the new baseball season. We have the privilege of playing the first game of the day. Everyone will be watching and history will record what takes place here today. Now, during this last winter break several rules have been changed for the good of THE GAME."

When the manager said THE GAME everyone stood up, took their caps off and held them over their hearts. It had long become the patriotic thing to do, but only if people felt like doing it. Everyone felt like doing it, so everyone did it.

"Okay, sit down. ... There are three rule changes used today for the first time in the history of league baseball. The outcry of the individual fans and the consensus of public opinion have dictated these new rules. The league officials, team owners and your ACLUE union leaders have written up these changes and included them in the official rulebook for baseball. This was all done for the good of THE GAME."

"Okay, sit down. ... I am well aware that you know these three new rules, but just so we are all up to speed, let me review them with you. Rule #1 is the "Reverse Newton Rule." The offensive team shall not be allowed to put the ball in play such that gravitation has an effect on the ball. Rule #2 is the "Time's-Out

Rule." The defensive team shall not be permitted to use time. And finally, Rule #3 is the so-called "Permissive Rule." The umpires, when enforcing the rules, will be guided by simple tolerance. I am sure, if we all work together, these rules will be for the good of THE GAME."

"Okay, sit down. ... Are there any questions? If there are, ask your ACLUE leaders. For those of you who opted not to be union members, you don't have ACLUE. You will submit your questions in writing and have them answered by league officials. Now, let's go out there and play like this is the last game of the season and we need a win to clinch the pennant."

A great shout went forth and the team members filed out of the locker room and onto the field. The fans greeted the hometown team with a rousing cheer, although a few fans expressed disapproval via the customary jeers and gestures.

The first batter was #24 and he took the first pitch, a strike on the outside corner of the plate. He checked the third base coach who was giving the coded signs. The second pitch was a ball outside. The batter hit the third pitch, but got underneath it. The ball went high over the pitcher into short center field. Just as the pop fly began to come down the second base umpire yelled, "You're out!" A second or so later the shortstop made the catch. The third base coach and #24 looked at each other in dismay. The coach walked out to speak with the umpire.

"Look partner, I know it's the first game, first batter and all, but please wait to call the guy out until the catch is made, okay?"

The umpire said to the coach, "Listen. Your player was out before the catch was made."

"Whaddya mean, 'before the catch was made'?"

The ump continued, "It's the Reverse Newton Rule. If what goes up starts to come down, then the offensive team has violated the new rule about gravity. So, when your player hit the ball and the ball changed course in the air because of gravity, he's out. Simple as that."

"What?"

Two old timers in the stands were trying to figure out what had just happened. The man wearing the mauve baseball cap asked the man with the first baseperson's glove, "What happened?"

The man with the first baseperson's glove said, "I dunno."

Over the public address system the announcement was made, "The batter was called out by the Reverse Newton Rule."

"Ohhhh," said the two elderly fans in unison.

The umpire politely said to the coach, "Please go back to your coaching box, and let's play THE GAME."

After the players put their caps back on and the two fans sat down, the next batter, #11, stepped to the plate. She was an aggressive lefty. She took two strikes and then smashed a screaming line drive right at the pitcher. The ball hit him in the glove and dropped to the ground in front of the pitcher. He picked it up and threw the batter out by eight steps. The umpire did his imitation of a single-winged aircraft and made the call, "Safe!"

There was a second of stunned, silent, disbelief from both fans and players. The pitcher recovered from the shock and ran to confront the first base umpire. "Safe? What are you talking about. The ball got to the base way before she did. She didn't even get to the bag until after you called her safe. What's the matter with you? Are you crazy?"

The first base umpire, with an attitude of confident patience, replied, "I thought so. I knew it would be like this and so I could only anticipate calling her safe. You see, as a member of the defensive team you are obliged not to break the Time's Out Rule; which of course you broke. Your confession of the intent to the use of time in getting the runner out only confirmed--"

"My confession of the intent to the use of time?"

"Yes, when you used the words *before* and *after*, you confessed to your time-intent for getting the runner out. When you violated that rule, the batter is obviously safe."

Four other infielders and the manager of the defensive team joined the bewildered pitcher. The pitcher continued his complaint, "What are you talking about? The ball got there *before* she did. Or, if it helps you, she got there *after* the ball did."

"Exactly. Thank you very much for those kind, affirming words. Wow, I did make a great call!"

"Look, change that call, you jerk. She's out!"

The umpire remained unconvinced, "Sorry, but you violated the rule that deals with time. *Before* and *after* are time terms and you cannot use them. Please remember, 'Time's Out for the defensive team.' You have to make the outs without using time. So don't come over here trying to appeal the call by using words like *before, after, while* or *when*. She is awarded first base as an out-runner."

The manager dropped his head and looked over his glasses at the ump. "A, uh ... out-runner?"

"Yes, an out-runner. She is out, but still has the right to run the bases. Even though she is out, the out doesn't count as one of the three outs in the inning. If she scores a run, it, of course, quite naturally, probably does not count. Awarding the status of out-runner to a batter is up to the discretion of the umpire. It wouldn't be right to break her spirit and repress her expressions of THE GAME by calling her out and then, adding insult to injury, not permitting her to run. And besides, I really felt like making this call at this time."

The pitcher walked to the dugout and shouted the announcement to one of the assistant coaches, "She's an out-runner."

The man with the mauve baseball cap asked the man with the first baseperson's glove, "Whattsa out-runner?"

The man with the first baseperson's glove said, "I dunno."

Over the public address system the announcement was made, "An out-runner is an offensive player who has been the object of a Time's Out Rule infraction by one or more members of the defensive team. The batter is out, but still allowed to run, if and only if, the umpire feels like allowing the batter to run. Neither the out counts nor the run, if and when, the out-runner scores. Probably."

"Ohhhh," said the two elderly fans in unison.

"Next batter," shouted the home plate umpire.

Up stepped #31. When the pitcher went into the stretch, the out-runner broke for second. The pitcher watched her make it to second without sliding. Then he delivered the pitch. Ball, too high. The catcher fired the ball back to the pitcher. At the moment he caught the ball, the pitcher raced to first base and tagged it. "You're out, #31," howled the umpire and thumbed her out of the batter's box and to the dugout.

"Time," requested the first base coach.

"Time out," replied the first base ump.

The coach looked at the umpire in disbelief. "The ball wasn't in play. What is going on here?"

The umpire gave a nodding approval to the pitcher and said, "You're beginning to understand, aren't you?"

The pitcher responded, "Yes. I ran over to first and tagged the bag. In doing so, I didn't violate the Time's Out Rule. And calling her out was a judgment call by the umpire. Right?"

"You got it," answered the ump.

The man with the mauve baseball cap asked the man with the first baseperson's glove, "What happened?"

The man with the first baseperson's glove said, "I dunno."

Over the public address system the announcement was made, "The Time's Out Rule was not violated."

"Ohhhh," said the two fans in unison.

"Let's go," said the head umpire, "let's get on with THE GAME."

For the first time in so long a time that no one could remember since when or for how long, not all of the ball players took off caps and covered their hearts. The shortstop was talking with the third base coach and the center fielder. The first base umpire joked with the pitcher and the catcher. A significant number of fans remained seated, prompting others to boo. A number of heated discussions ensued and a few altercations broke out in the stands. Some fans began to file out of the ballpark.

The managers finally got the game going again. The next batter was #2, a scrawny, ten-year-old kid. The pitcher started his delivery and then stopped suddenly. "Balk," cried the home plate umpire, waving the out-runner to third. The kid walked on the next four pitches. That left one out, one runner on and one out-runner left on, and it was still the top of the first.

A woman, #20, came up to the plate and walked on four pitches. Instead of going to first, she went to third claiming to the umpire that the Tolerance Rule ought to apply. The umpire, being a permissive man, agreed. That meant that two women were on third base, which was quite scandalous. In days passed, only husband-wife couples had been allowed to round the bases and run home together. Now, abandoning the absolute rules of THE GAME even fans, players and umpires openly promoted two men or two women on the same base. What was once a strict taboo based upon the original creator's design of THE GAME was now another corrupted part of the sport, brought in based on the consensus of human opinion and supported by the popular opinion polls. Those devoted to THE GAME began to speculate concerning when the consensus of human opinion would favor putting children on base with adults. At the present rate of decay, same base pedoplay would soon be acceptable within the culture of THE GAME.

The next batter, a seven-year-old girl in pigtails, was called out on strikes. The man on-deck was huge and swung a lead-filled pipe in order to prepare for his turn at bat. He stepped to the plate, eyed the pitcher and crushed the ball with such power that it was still ascending when it left the park. It came down near a set of railroad tracks more than 500 feet away from home plate. The umpire's eye watched carefully and when convinced that the towering shot had begun to come down called the batter out. The Reverse Newton Rule once again claimed a victim.

The top of the first inning took nearly an hour to play. The bottom of the inning never started. Ball players were standing in small groups arguing calls made in the top of the inning. Two players watched as an ACLUE union leader wrote something on a pad of paper. There were only sparse pockets of fans in the stands. Most of the people had abandoned THE GAME after the first forty minutes of play.

The end of THE GAME was sealed when an ACLUE official and two animal rights advocates brought a donkey onto the field with the expectation that the animal would be able to pinch run or at least to call strikes behind home plate. The manager of the home team protested saying that one jackass behind the plate was enough. With that the umpires left. Then the outfielders threw down their gloves and walked off the field. The two women stayed on third base waiting for the first opportunity to go home together.

The man with the mauve baseball cap asked the man with the first baseperson's glove, "What happened?"

The man with the first baseperson's glove said, "The ever-widening gap between the original design of THE GAME's creator and the corruption of said design by means of the disregard for the reality of time and the neglect of the law of gravity, coupled with the entropic consensus of popular human opinion have rendered an irreparable tear in the fabric of THE GAME resulting in the irreversible degeneration of the rules, the impending collapse of order and the ultimate destruction of THE GAME."

Startled and taken back by the answer, the man wearing the mauve baseball cap asked, "What did you say?"

The man with the first baseperson's glove said, "I dunno."

Over the public address system the announcement was made, "They've called THE GAME."

Standing, taking off their caps and covering their hearts, the two elderly fans, the only fans remaining, said in unison, "Ohhhh."

CHAPTER 8

ASCENSION

Once again I woke with a start, as if tardy, as if compelled to catch up with a schedule imposed on me. Anxiety mixed with panic and produced an impulse to hurried activity. Pain checked any sudden movement. While the pillow supported my neck, the back of my head rested directly on the floor of the loft. The resultant flat spot on my skull throbbed. A crick in my neck caused pain as I turned to the side. In addition, the rough plank floor had rendered no mercy to my back during the night. My throat was dry and the first swallow stuck at midpoint.

The woman and the boy were gone. I thought my snoring might have forced them from their sleeping bags. Regret for not having invested time with them motivated me to correct my negligence. Anticipating a painful descent on the ladder due to tender feet, I slipped into my boots for protection from the sharp rungs. Taking care not to step on the loose laces, I quickly made my way down the ladder. No one was in the kitchen.

On my way outside, a glance into the corner of the stall informed me that Chameleon had left during the night or early morning. His absence did not trouble me until a moment of panic prompted quicker steps to the entryway. I was running when the morning sun struck my face and I stumbled to a halt. Panning left to right revealed Chameleon standing in the shadow of a large tree. From the other side of the stream, Gabby looked in my direction, his head slightly tilted. He appeared concerned, but it was difficult to tell from this distance. Honestly, I did not care.

The concern I did have was the location of the woman and the boy. The cool, morning air invigorated me and cleared my mind. Chameleon remained in the shadow of the tree. He leaned back with his arms dangling. The morning sun projecting from the far side of the large tree, made it difficult to see much of him in the shadows. Frankly, I did not care.

He spoke with a tone of optimism, "She left you a note."

Without thanking or acknowledging him, I turned back to the shelter and found the note in the kitchen.

> *There's a change of clothes on the shelf. The boy and I had a great time yesterday. We decided to do the same today at a waterfall we saw, but didn't have time to explore. Hope you don't mind. We had to leave early.*
>
> *Love you,*
> *Me*
>
> *p.s. You were snoring!*

The note was not a disappointment for me. In fact, a welcomed sense of relief welled up, lessening the guilty feelings. This excused conscience permitted me to follow a yearning for something yet unknown. Even though no clear knowledge of either destination or route could be discerned, I felt drawn and compelled elsewhere. I changed clothes and returned to the morning outside the cabin.

Anticipating the whole day to myself, I wanted to lock out any thought that would cast a pall on the day or anyone who would cause me delay. That's when I noticed Chameleon's presence in the shadows. I determined to deal with him succinctly.

Confidently, I walked to him and demanded, "Chameleon, is intolerance to be tolerated?"

"Please, my friend, say some more about this."

"You're always playing the part; always trying to get more information in order to be what I want you to be. You will have no success this morning. None. You need to answer the question. In fact, you're too late. I have withdrawn the query and am no longer interested in that answer. So, tell me, how is it that you have healed so quickly? That really seems quite unnatural to me, considering the severity of your wounds. Are you sure that you are better?"

"Perhaps I am not as well as I appear to be. In fact -"

"Save it. You're too late, Chameleon. A simple *yes* or *no* would have satisfied me. I am no longer curious about your condition. I must say good-by now, so, 'Good-by'."

Without waiting for his reply, I turned and walked to the creek.

Chameleon called out, "I'll see you later."

His manner of speaking bothered me. His voice gave no hint that he uttered an empty phrase. On the contrary, he spoke in a manner that was declaratory. I admonished myself for letting him get to me, even in this small way. My face had been set in the direction of the camp across the creek where I hoped for an invitation to Gabby's breakfast table.

My attitude changed as I negotiated the small stream. I thought about Tetra Graham. He evoked fear and dislike from me. Chameleon moved me from involved compassion to repugnant apathy. Gabby was different and my confidence waned as I approached his camp. While with Gabby a feeling of unworthiness and a sense of demotion overcame me. I supposed it was because of his warm welcome and satisfying meals, but it seemed more than these things. He welcomed me but an unidentifiable lack of comfort or worthiness in me existed. I felt at peace when with him, and at the same time, I experienced some uneasiness.

The pleasant creek was rather wide, but not especially deep. The high water marks on the nearby trees made me wonder if this stream ever became a raging flood as to reach such a height.

It seemed unlikely so high on this mountain, but the objective evidence of the high standard existed on those trees.

"Good morning, Gabby."

"And also to you."

He handed me a plate with ample portions of ham, eggs, biscuits and cheese. As I added the salt and pepper, he poured a cup of coffee and placed it next to me. The breakfast satisfied as any meal I could recall. After eating, Gabby exchanged my plate for a second cup of coffee.

"Gabby, what a fine breakfast! Thank you so much."

"You are welcome. While you finish your coffee I will put these things away. We will then be ready."

He spoke in a factual manner.

"Ready for what?"

I recalled our parting words last night, remembered my thoughts before going to sleep and pondered the rather bizarre dream. A dark mesh covered my mind and I sighed. Did we really have to proceed with depressing discussions on this splendid morning? I tried to keep him and his discussions at arm's length, doing so with a cavalier attitude.

"Oh yes, I would like to talk with you about the positions held by Chameleon and Tetra Graham, but perhaps later. I really want to get away from here, maybe take a short hike up the mountain."

Gabby continued without breaking stride in his preparations, "Yes, I know. However, before leaving, we must get ready. Certain preparatory tasks need to be completed."

Gabby stepped inside his tent and returned a moment later with a hiking pack that he hoisted onto his back and shoulders.

"I'm set. Are you ready?"

Once again frustration and anger surfaced. Was he simply an old man who wanted to tag along? Not a chance of that since he assumed the role of leading. Would I now seem ungrateful if I told him I preferred being alone? As the apparent refrain for the day, guilt rose within me at the thought of neither permitting him to come along with me nor letting him take charge. Nonetheless, I attempted diplomatically to distance myself from him.

"Hey, Gabby, I'm just going for a hike today. I'm not even really sure where."

"When you go up the mountain, you are not just hiking for the day."

"Look, Gabby, I have no particular destination."

"Yes, you do."

He spoke with conviction and without eye contact as he adjusted a pack strap. I wanted to snap at him, but instead, all that came out was a mocking, "Well, sire, please tell me where we are going."

Without hesitation or apparent irritation, he replied, "Up the mountain. But in order to get there we must begin."

I started walking to the timberline and asked, "Very good, and you would like to come along?"

"There are four reasons why I must accompany you. Before you ask me what they are, you must know that three of them will be revealed later. As for the first, it is necessary to speak with you as we hike."

I wanted to ask him what the topic of conversation might be, but hesitated, knowing he would tell me even if I did not ask. Therefore I replied, "You make it sound as if you were under orders."

"I am."

"Whose?"

"The one who sent me."

"The one who sent you?"

"Yes."

Gabby's short answer indicated he did not want to pursue this. As we passed from the tree line, I attempted to reconstruct my thoughts from the previous night. In order to find out who Chameleon and Tetra Graham were, I had to discover what each one believed.

96

"Well then, Gabby, it is quite certain that you know more than I do. So please talk to me. I need to determine which of those two is telling me the truth. Tell me, Gabby, which one represents the truth? What are my options?"

Short and terse, without hesitating at hearing my words, as if he knew what I would ask and had rehearsed his response, he answered, "You have two."

More than a bit frustrated, I said with no small hint of sarcasm, "Well, that seems obvious."

"Not necessarily."

Irritated, I replied, "Well, it sure does Gabby! Either it is Tetra Graham and his cold, legalistic objectivity, or Chameleon and his warm, ever-changing standards. What else is there that could be said about them?"

"Much could be said. However, you are pursuing two dead end options. Those two you mention are not the only two alternatives. There are at least four scenarios."

"I thought you said I had two options?"

"You do have two. However, there are two more, and possibly three, that you don't have because you haven't thought of them."

Wanting to get further with the conversation, I besought him, "Or, haven't been told about them. Please, Gabby, tell me of your two new options."

"They are not mine, but yours. The first is that you choose neither of the two proposals, and the second is like it, that you accept both of the teachings. A third is your continuation in the planned promise that rejects both of the previous two systems of thought and practice while acknowledging and confessing the one who perfectly fulfilled the standard. This is the way that you have known from childhood."

"Gabby, what are you talking about?"

"I speak of the objective promise that is of no benefit to you unless it is heard and you are drawn to it."

Gabby spoke without interruption of his breathing as we hiked. Because of the pace as well as the need to hold my peace, I took a deep breath, stopped and turned to look down the mountain. In the short time of our walk we had already passed through the area that had been the darkest the night before, the depression I termed the valley of the shadows. The area was disturbing in the dark. Now, with the light shining into the valley, nothing was hidden. Silently I chided myself for having such fears the previous night. The terrors of the night diminish when considered and viewed in the light of day.

Frustration turned to bewilderment and my response followed, "Let me put what you said in different terms. I should either reject what both of them are saying, or accept as true what they both claim, or discover a way I already know. Am I close here? Am I in the ballpark?"

"You are getting closer. You still have a long way to go. So come, while we are able. Let us continue our hiking."

His selection of pronouns did not go unnoticed and was, by that time, not unexpected. In truth, there was actually a degree of comfort in what he said.

The climb continued. I positioned myself to the left of Gabby with reason; he would be closer to the edge of the invisible cliff. I felt no shame in doing this. If the cliff were to appear suddenly, then he would be the one standing on the solid shelf of thin air. In reality, my positioning became academic. The course chosen by Gabby tended more to the east than where I had stood yesterday. He had veered across the line because he wanted me to be over the edge as well.

We hiked for a couple hours. Scrub bushes became sparse and soon disappeared. At higher elevations, glacial rubble and wind-blown sand collected between the larger rocks. Fields of large, sloughed rock were encountered and left behind. We approached the real crevasse, the one that could be seen to the east.

We said nothing during this time. I attempted to think about everything said by the three strangers; Tetra Graham, Gabby and Chameleon. There were too many unknowns. I needed to hear more from them, though the only one I somewhat cared to be with was Gabby. Even in his company, doubts surfaced. Did Gabby deceive me? Did I really want to speak with the other two? As the air thinned, thinking became increasingly difficult. The climbing clouded my focus and sapped my energy. Soon I put one foot in front of the other and cast a tired, continuous, stupefying gaze at the ground.

Near the edge of the ravine Gabby stopped. Despite the pace of the hike and his heavy pack, this older man did not gasp for air as I continued to do. His arms folded back as he shed the pack. He placed it on the ground and looked down the mountain.

He asked, "Have you been looking back at all this morning?"

"No. I guess I should have been, but you know the way."

Without acknowledging my response, he continued in that matter-of-fact manner that irritated me, "Here is where you go on alone. Now, look back down ..."

"Wait a minute, Gabby, what are you talking about?"

"What I mean to do is give you enough of a bearing to keep you from getting lost. Please pay attention. The second reason for my being here is to show you the way you have come and the way you are to go. Now please, look back toward camp. When you return, aim for the depression and always keep the dark green stand of timber down there to your right. That means you must stay to the left as you return. If you don't, the lay of the mountain will force you into the western ravine."

"Why can't you go with me? Besides, who says that I am even going to continue? In fact, I'm just as likely to return to camp with you. After all, this is just a day hike."

As usual, my words did not deter Gabby. He turned, looked up the mountain slope to the northwest and continued, "That outcropping of rock is where you are going. Around the base, along the underside is a cleft in the rock. You will be able to go inside there and be protected from the cold temperatures and the adverse weather conditions. To get there you must follow this ravine up the mountain until you are at the same elevation as the outcropping. Then traverse the snowfield to the outcropping."

There seemed to be no stopping him. He determined to tell me where I would go and how I would get there. I raised a final objection, "Enough! You don't seem to realize that I am not going up there. I don't have the proper gear. I have no food, no water -"

"The third reason I came along this far was to bear your pack to this point. Whatever you need is in the pack. There is a coat, a hat, a pair of gloves, a canteen of water, dried fruit and some matches, though it does not seem likely you will find anything to burn."

I attempted to raise another final objection, though in doing so I admitted my resignation, "What about gear for going across the glacier? There isn't even a snow axe. It just isn't smart to get into something like that without the proper equipment, Gabby."

"As long as you do not attempt to cross the snowfield until you are at the same elevation as the outcropping there is no danger and you will arrive in time. The area to be crossed is fairly level. If you fall down, you will not slide. Do you want me to go over any of these details again?"

"No. Please recall that I didn't ask to hear about any of them in the first place."

"I will go over them for you, if you are unclear about any of the things I have told you."

"No, but answer me this, what is the fourth reason that you are here?"

"This is neither the place nor the time for you to know. Knowing some things ahead of time is not helpful. The reason will be evident to you when the time comes and you are in the place where the revelation will take place. The pack is provided, but it does you no good if you refuse it. Within the pack are items intended to be a blessing to you. You are capable of having all the blessings in your pack and on your back. You are able to bear the pack and the rest of the entire burden in your journey and still die because the food that satisfies your hunger is ignored, the water that slakes your thirst is denied, the clothing that covers is neglected and the light that reveals remains potential energy."

He smiled. I snarled. He held out the pack. I formally submitted. He hoisted the pack onto my back. He sat on a boulder and faced away from me and down the mountain. Muttering to myself I began trudging up the mountain once more with the ravine some thirty feet to the east. I spat on the ground in protest of the hike behind. Really, what authority did Gabby have over me? None. I spit on the ground in protest of the hike ahead. But then, why had I been traipsing up this mountain for the last five minutes all by myself, and why was I continuing to ascend? At that moment my feet stopped. I turned to yell at Gabby. I hadn't determined what I would say quite yet, but it would come to me.

The problem remained unresolved, for after gazing back, there was no trace of Gabby. I had not hiked that far and it had not been that long since I left him sitting on the rock. I didn't remember any place where he might be able to hide. However, there must have been since I wouldn't believe that he had disappeared into the thin air or that he suddenly became invisible. A wave of frustration, conceived in anger and growing in fearful momentum, quickly overwhelmed me. The only reasonable thing to do was return to the cabin. True, I thought, but I also felt under orders and compelled in the journey. Therefore the hike upward and the march onward continued.

I asked myself in a mumble, "How long would it take me to get to the outcropping?"

Ahead and slightly to the right, that is, across the ravine and high on the opposite snowfield, a dark spot descended. I thought it might be someone skiing that snowfield or taking a sled down its slope. While both possibilities seemed unlikely, I had no other explanation.

I spoke aloud, "Let's say it takes me another three hours to get to the big rock area. I could touch the base and return to this spot in three more hours."

Whatever that dark creature was doing on the distant snowfield, it was definitely not sliding. Actually, it appeared to be running, though it certainly did not seem human.

I muttered, "When I get back to this point the hike down will be about two to three more hours, maybe a bit shorter since the return trip is downhill."

It appeared to be an animal. A wolf? Coyote? Mountain lion? No, a dog! What was a dog doing way up here? The animal appeared to be running in my general direction.

"Anyway, let's say it's ten o'clock now ... three there ... three back ... two to camp. That's eight hours, putting me back into camp at six this evening."

The dog ran to the edge of the ravine and stopped. The distance between us seemed no more than two or three hundred feet. He looked at me and raised his nose in the air as if to get my scent. He was a hound of some type. Even from this distance, I could tell he had an anxious, concerned manner about him, as if he were my servant, a best friend who earnestly wanted to come to me.

I continued speaking aloud and to myself, "Darkness will be covering the mountain at six. That would mean having to go through the valley of the shadows once more. Is it possible to make up time by jogging across the snowfield and arriving at the valley before it would be completely dark?"

The hound looked at me, ran to the edge, hesitated a moment and then bound down the steep ravine. In an instant he fell out of my view. Quickly I moved to a safe point, a secure place within a few feet of the ravine's edge. A small avalanche of gravel and larger rocks consumed the dog. As the mass slid, huge boulders became dislodged and joined the avalanche. Dust clouds billowed, obscuring any view. Thundering smashes of boulder crashing into boulder added to and overwhelmed the sound of grating gravel. Echoes heightened the already deafening noise caused by the plastic flow. The rumble continued for nearly a minute as the hound was carried away to its death, buried in the abyss of the ravine. Then all was quiet and the only sign of anything having ever occurred was the boiling waves of rock dust. I waited to hear something, hoping to hear some noise. After considering all these things, I concluded it was better not to hear any call from the depths below me.

Panic rose within me as my attention turned from the hound to myself. The edge of the ravine, a short two feet in front of me, conjured haunting thoughts of the invisible cliff and Tetra Graham. Heights had always been troublesome for me, especially at the edge of a precipice or on a narrow mountain trail. At such times, my imagination took over even when all conditions were safe.

I backed a few feet from the edge, knowing that turning around at the edge would be quite foolish. The twisting of my ankle while pivoting or the sudden over-balancing of the bulky pack could easily send me over the ledge. Even if I survived the fall and reached the bottom without serious injury, the valley would be a prison. Escape would be impossible. In fact, a fallen prisoner, trapped in the valley of such a place, might reasonably pray for any overhang above him to break loose and hasten his death.

Having scooted a safe distance from the edge of the ravine, I stood and continued my trek. The pack became heavier and my head hung lower. Two hours were spent. The thinner air became sharper as I drew deeper breaths. Attempting to pick up the pace only caused my lungs to burn. The higher areas of ground were characterized by small, solid rock formations, some of which required short climbs.

To the west the rock outcropping stood like a sentinel. I was not quite at the same elevation, though close enough, I thought, to cross at this point. The wind picked up. The effects of the horizontal hike replacing the climb were noticed immediately.

The hiking became easier. My energy output decreased. I cooled. The snowfield remained a quarter mile ahead. Ten minutes later the temperature had dropped several more degrees. Both the wind blowing across the snow, as well as the thought of the wind blowing across the snow, chilled me.

I wiggled out of the pack and let it drop to the ground. Loosening the straps and peeling back the top flap revealed Gabby's coat. A grateful smile crossed my face as I put it on. I opened the canteen and took a long drink. The cool water outlined my rib cage. A side pocket yielded dried fruit, including quartered pears, sliced apples, banana chips, and something that looked like rhubarb. I would save the food. With the straps adjusted for the additional layer of Gabby's coat and the pack hoisted into place, the trek continued.

Slushy glacial ice characterized the edge of the snowfield. As I took the first steps on the melting snow, my boots sank until they found a solid base six inches below the surface. Ten feet from the edge, the colder snow had crusted enough to prevent me from sinking more than an inch or two.

For two hundred feet the snowfield ascended slightly but not enough for the inclination to be dangerous. Beyond that, however, the lay of the snowfield changed. A steeper slope fell away and down to the left. The mound ahead and to the right rose ominously. Only the top of the rock outcropping could be seen from where I stood. I had attempted the crossover too soon and had two alternatives, to continue across the perilous snowfield ahead or to begin climbing the snowfield to my right. Retracing my steps to the edge of the ravine was not an option. Whether for good or bad, retreat had never been either the inclination or the practice in my life. It would not begin now. Brute force, bullheaded stubbornness and sage ignorance combined once again to prevent my going back.

The ascent to the right continued. At first, the footing remained manageable. My rate of travel in this dangerous snowfield slowed from a hiking pace to a climbing one. I chastised myself for not having taken Gabby's advice and berated myself for a lack of personal discipline. While resting at one point and putting on Gabby's thick coat for protection, I directed a personal slur at the pushy old man.

Gradually the sentinel became visible beyond the massive knoll of snow. This rock remained the only indication of where the top edge of the mound crested. The line separating the top of the snowfield and the sky above could no longer be detected. The gray sky nearly matched the milky snowfield and mound. The clouds were banking against the mountain, the wind was increasing and a storm began bearing down on me.

An hour later it was safe to begin the trek across the remaining section. My imagination continued to question the safety of this crossing. Again Gabby had been right; there was no danger of sliding at this point. But how did I know that this snowfield might not be a thin ice-bridge across some great chasm? I thought about such catastrophes. Would the crust below me break away? At any moment I might fall through and into a crevasse extending for hundreds of feet. I knew there would come a time when such a snow-bridge would give way. Why not now, especially since I stood at its center? I stepped lightly.

The fur-lined gloves protected my hands and the hat flaps covered my ears. Gusts swirled around the sentinel and descended on me. The wind blew where it willed and it willed blowing against me. I turned my coat collar up and fastened its top button. The sleet began and struck me from a nearly horizontal angle.

Reaching the outcropping of rock seemed my only hope. The wind and freezing rain pellets prevented me from lifting my eyes. Except for an occasional peak at the rock for direction, I bowed my head as I walked. The stone sentinel loomed ahead of me. How small it appeared at a distance. How massive and out of proportion the outcropping grew as I approached. The temperature continued to plummet. The last few steps on the snowfield were not slushy as they had been on the other side. Ice pellets became projectiles skipping across the drifts and smashing into any obstacles, myself included. Horizontally propelled by the stormy blast, these frozen missiles collided and bounced until coming to rest in shadowy, wind-protected pockets.

Thirty minutes later I arrived at the base of the sentinel. I found it impossible to locate a seam and determine where the base of this rock outcropping actually began. The mountain and the rock were one.

The granular pellets changed to fine snow and clouds billowed and swirled around me. Visibility was reduced to a few feet. The cleft would have to be found soon. I inched my way around the lower edge of the rock formation. A hundred feet took ten minutes to travel.

I wondered how I would recognize this cleft. I was in serious trouble and could die from exposure looking for the place of safety. Gabby had led me astray. Evaluating my strength, I concluded that my time left on earth consisted only of minutes. I invoked another personal curse upon Gabby. Perhaps no cleft existed.

A fierce gust of wind forced me to turn my face, to lean my body against the rock. Another blast came from the slope below driving my face upward. I opened my eyes to maintain my balance. There, five feet above me, was a ledge. The cleft began at that point. I had naively thought I would discover the cleft by strolling around the base and into the cleft, similar to the way a walk-in wardrobe is entered. With hands and feet that were not particularly nimble at this point, I somehow managed to maneuver my way up to the cleft. The floor of the cleft was narrow and uneven. Because the cleft was protected from the storm's fiercest winds, the snow fell in a gentler manner. An inch of snow and ice, possibly more, had accumulated on the cleft floor. This crease in the sentinel's bulk sheltered me from the full force of the storm. Behind me the raging blizzard continued. Ahead I could see the cleft extended farther. Around a slight turn and some twenty feet beyond, the passageway ended. In this blocked, rock hallway, where there was protection from the icy, horrific blasts of winds, minutes of remaining life might be extended to a few hours.

The wind howled certain death and chased me farther into the cleft until the miniature box canyon stopped me. Now I envisioned myself huddled and waiting to fall asleep for the last time in this world. It is strange, but I thought about which way to face, whether to sit facing anyone who might walk into the cleft, or to die with my back to the world.

In the midst of such contemplation about the position of death and the messages communicated by them, I saw, three feet above the path's end, a large triangular opening, a hole in the wall. Light extended several feet and I saw this would be a place where I could not only be further protected from the blasting wind, but shielded from the snow and bitter cold. Shedding the pack from one shoulder, I climbed through the entryway. I discovered the entrance to be the smallest part of this hole. The size of the room increased as I peered deeper within the cave. It went farther back with a rough, floored area that sloped away slightly from the entrance.

I perched inside the entrance of the cave. My mind conjured images of mountain lions, hibernating bears and hungry wolves. I remained still, focusing my eyes into the darkness at the back of the cave. My nose could detect no smell giving the hint of any animal hiding within. My ears strained to hear something, but nothing sounded forth. Several minutes later my eyes discerned the interior of the cave. The corridor was high enough for me to stand, but not without bending over. It was wide enough for two people to pass each other, but not without difficulty. Fifteen to twenty feet from the entrance was a bowl-shaped room.

For refuge, I moved to the back of the cave and placed my pack in the center of the small room. I located matches in a side pocket and struck one on the wall of the cave. Light flooded the cave and confirmed I was alone. Even the expected ring of stones where cavemen had built a fire was missing. No wood at all; no debris; no sign that any human being or animal had ever been inside. As far as I could determine, nobody had ever been in this tomb. It was the same as the day it had been hewn and could have been formed thousands of years ago or yesterday.

When the match went out there was complete darkness once again. Slowly the entrance became visible. Outside it continued to snow heavily. When my eyes had adjusted, I dug into the pack and brought out a lightweight blanket and a smaller cloth. The blanket would be big enough to put under me as well as wrap around my body. The smaller cloth would serve as a cushion or as a covering for my head. I drank from the canteen and set it to my right side. Reaching deeper, I discovered a first aid kit and returned it to its place. I found other packages of dried fruit. My sense of smell helped me identify the dried pears and apples that became part of my meal. One bag contained a large handful of dried cherries. A biscuit, one of two evidently left over from breakfast, concluded the meal. Another drink from the canteen washed everything down.

Immediately after eating, I scolded myself, "You have no idea how long it is going to take to wait out this storm. You have no inventory of your food supplies. You should have made a plan for rationing your food and water. Your half-empty canteen bears witness against you."

I became drowsy. I guessed the time to be no earlier than 4:00 and no later than 5:00pm. I spread the blanket out and wrapped it around me. The soft side of the pack served as a makeshift support for my back. Outside the storm raged, the wind howled and the snow continued to accumulate. Inside I found peace and quiet, and indeed, an opportunity for rest. Within minutes I fell asleep.

CHAPTER 9

CHOOSE THIS NIGHT

Thirst and hunger were the first companions to greet me upon awakening. Considering the exertion of the climb, I expected the thirst. The hunger pangs surprised me and their presence indicated that four or five hours must have elapsed during my restful sleep to cause me such hunger. My eyes remained closed even after I awakened. I had no particular reason to open them at the midnight hour. My sleeping posture remained comfortable as I slept and continued in the position as I huddled in the dark hole.

This allowed for a curious contemplation. What is man that Thou art mindful of him? I imagined the layers of a large onion. But rather than considering the onion from the outside in and peeling away its layers to get to the core, I began at the center and worked my way through the outer layers.

My thoughts and what made me an aware, conscious, sentient, living being were somewhere dashing about within me, that is, within my mind. However, as I thought on this I realized that the mind was of a non-physical dimension of reality contained within and conjoined to my brain. This mystical union, with the brain the host and the mind the guest, is what made me, me. Here within, at the center of the onion, was the seed, seat and soul of who I was and who I am.

My brain is neatly and creatively encased in my skull. The skull is part of the package known as the body, both of which are covered by skin. I am wearing clothes, another layer. My clothed body is a chrysalis wrapped in a blanket. The blanket about me is the outer layer of my cocoon. This cocoon is now nestled in this hole in a mountain, which itself is immersed in clouds and encased in the earth's atmosphere. This planet remains a tiny speck in a small solar system implanted on the universal womb. How insignificant this made me. And yet, who am I that Thou art mindful of me? How many, like me, alone in the caves of life, have had these same thoughts? Had they felt as small and alone as I ...

At that instant an invasion took place in one of those many layers and I became intuitively, instinctively and intensely aware of the visitation. The invasion was undetected by either ear or eye or any sense commonly used. Nevertheless, and with no doubt, one of the other senses communicated to me that someone or something was in the cave. I sensed a coolness without degree, a communion without presence, as if at the same time, no one and someone were here.

My heart raced and my five senses heightened, the latter whetted and alert for receiving information. I feared being contacted by the other one who most certainly was with me in the cave. Though I had not been touched, the other presence pressed me. I did not stir. Darkness continued. I opened my mouth and detected no unusual tastes. Only the continual, cooling silence sounded in the cave. No smells could be detected. Still, I was not alone.

What were the possibilities? Gabby seemed the best possibility and my first, logical hope. He sent me here and knew where I would be. Perhaps he had followed me to make sure I found the cave. Yes indeed, Gabby. However, I doubted. It could be the slippery Chameleon or even the hardened Tetra Graham. Or, another human being or perhaps an animal sought refuge from the storm and entered the cave.

By rolling slightly and coughing loudly, I undertook a test to discover more about the visitor. If my fellow cave dweller did not previously know of my presence, he knew now. No growls, snarls or attacks followed my casual announcement. There was no scrambling to get out. My mind processed the test results and wondered how long an animal or a human might remain silent, still and hidden. Frustrated and frightened, I called out in a desperate plea, "Gabby?"

A voice thundered back, reverberating off the walls, and coming from no identifiable place in the cave. It accosted me.

"Fool! Are you finished with your menial game? Do not even begin to hope that messenger boy is here. Even if he were, he would not be able to help you, you whimpering, sniveling, insignificant mass of human flesh."

I experienced what I am only able to describe as pure terror at that instant. My mouth and mind failed me as I sat in physical, mental, spiritual, emotional and psychological shock. Had I been able to speculate at this point, I might have wondered if my mind had temporarily separated from my brain.

Another voice, to my left, questioned softly, "If he is insignificant, then why have you come here to be with him?"

From my right came the response, "Shut-up or I will finish the job I began on you the other night. Most assuredly, you creepy lizard, judgment day is coming for you. But first, this one wrapped in a blanket must be processed. In this sorry world of choice, he must make a decision. Choose this night the one you will serve. Which way will it be for you? Have you decided for the way of desire or for the way of discipline? Desire or discipline? Which way is it to be?"

The volume of Tetra Graham's voice decreased enough for me to know he sat at the opposite side of the dark cave from Chameleon. I moistened my mouth, swallowed and asked, "Are there no other choices?"

Chameleon immediately chimed in, "Yes, very good! Well done. Who says there are but two alternatives? Why not give him a few more selections from which he may choose what he desires?"

Tetra Graham directed his voice to Chameleon. "Reptile, you will speak only when spoken to."

The same voice was now aimed at me, "So, which will it be Maggot Fodder? ... self-denial or self-expression?"

"I don't understand."

"Quit stalling. Will it be the way of desire or the way of discipline? Are you going to follow the way you want things to be, letting your desires dictate what is true for a time? Or will you go the way of reality, acknowledging with your reason and possessing the way of historical truth and objective fact? Will you deny yourself and your expressions of personal belief, desire and hope? Or, will you go the way of the changing, decaying world, being driven by every cultural wind and each sui-societal fad that sings those seductive siren-songs? Speak up. It is finished. It is time!"

My heart raced and I shouted, "Leave me alone!"

He pushed, "Time's up! You must choose."

"Tetra Graham, you are intent on my deciding a way. Evidently, Chameleon does not find this so important. However, by choosing which way to go, am I not also determining which of you I will follow? Aren't I really deciding which of you will be ruler in and of my life?"

"Answer him, Tetra Graham, and answer him with all your objective truth."

"Silence, snake, or I will cause you to shed your skin before the time."

Chameleon responded in anger, "My body already bears many marks of your wrath. Your treatment of me has been atrocious and vindictive. And yet, oh Tetra Graham, I am still here. I have been around from the beginning and I will be here after the end. So, you sadistic and sorry excuse for incarnate malevolence, do not threaten me with either your vindictive words or your barbaric acts of cruelty."

"Well played, viper. Outstanding! This has been one of your most impressive performances yet."

Tetra Graham directed his voice to me once more, "Do you understand what happened here? This serpent has changed his skin to be what I want him to be. He has turned you against me by impersonating me. Have you bought it? Are you buying it?"

While I agreed with his position concerning absolute truths, Tetra Graham's practice was deplorable. He ran over others. The truth was everything, even at the expense of those who held it. He portrayed and lived a picture of rigid formalism. He advocated a judicial juggernaut. He was so certain in his stance that he was totally negative in his practice. His will demanded perfection; his practice imposed it. The code became the stick with which to beat out imperfection and to compel an admission of onerous doctrine. This standard practice became the burdensome activity that forces and fashions dogma into a negative confession of the truth. His pompous spirit and vindictive disregard for personal feelings were unacceptable.

At the same time, I knew Chameleon to be wrong in his theory. But his practice pleased so much that it was difficult to resist him. Once one became acquainted with Chameleon, he was easier to accept and this, of course, was dangerous. He called for all to be non-judgmental and loving. He pleaded a teaching and practice that respected another's choices and accepted their lifestyles. His manner and style appealed to those who make no distinction between freedom and license. His condemnation came only in two situations, first, for one who practiced the intolerance advocated by Tetra Graham and second, for one not choosing. One could be judgmental, narrow-minded and intolerant only so long as he neither preached nor imposed his will or choice on any one else. Any choice could be made, but a choice had to be made.

I resolved not to let either Tetra Graham or Chameleon know what I believed or what I was thinking. The best I could hope for was a debate that resulted in the two of them engaging in a sustained argument that placed me on the sidelines. Their hatred of one another should be used to my advantage. This became my strategy and would begin with an assault on Chameleon while distancing myself from Tetra Graham. Keeping the sides even and at arm's length, while maintaining the appearance of neutrality, would not be easy. Nevertheless, I continued.

8

"Tetra Graham, I believe you have avoided answering my question because you knew that my making a choice would be the same as choosing one of you to follow. I believe you have been as good and kind to me as you ever will be. With you, my situation will only get worse. Yours is a message without mercy and a program without pity. You appeal to the natural religion of man with its pagan ritual of bowing down to and appeasing the gods. You place before your victim the message of a standard and you wait. You do not want to sink the hook until the bait is taken."

Mentally, I was struggling.

"Continue," interrupted Tetra Graham, "you simpering man of anemic metaphors."

I was rejecting Tetra Graham and leaning to the position of Chameleon.

"However, there is also the possibility that I am capable of rejecting your discipleship while advocating the truth of some of your arguments; not that I am necessarily doing this you understand."

"Hah, Schwaffling One," grunted Tetra Graham, "you are imitating that stunted, deformed serpent right now. And it is a commendable performance, Little Chameleon. Why not voice with your anemic mouth the choice you have already made in your gutless heart?"

He was pressing me and I panicked. Seeking to divert his attention from me, I blurted out, "Tell me, Tetra Graham, do you change?"

"No, I am the same yesterday, today and tomorrow."

Then he laughed a deep, belly laugh and said, "Are you going to ask the rainbow lizard that question?"

I remained off-balance. So I tried again to gain time, "Tell me, Tetra Graham, is God the creator of evil?"

"No," he rifled back, "Now I insist, you must ask him the same question."

I thought the query posed to Tetra Graham concerning God and evil should have evoked more than a simple *no*. I had attempted to buy time with it and instead, everything was back in my lap too soon. I felt further trapped. Turning my head in the other direction, I asked, "Chameleon, is God the creator of evil?"

He sighed and said, "Please, give me a minute to formulate my thoughts."

Silently I thanked Chameleon for the extra time to think. It vanished as I contemplated what needed to be said. I also resented Chameleon because I felt indebted to him for his understanding my need for his time-delaying plea.

After a few moments he spoke, "You have asked me a question and you expect an answer. My request for time to consider both the question and part of my answer indicates it is an excellent question. But really, my friend, would you truly believe me if I answered it? I have endured mockery and abuse because of who I am. My friend, would you believe me if I fully answered your question?"

His honesty was appreciated. Consequently, I stated the truth to him, "Chameleon, I am not certain whether I would or not. But please, is God the creator of evil?"

"No," came his reply. He quickly added, "Do you believe me?"

"I don't know. However there are two consolations I have. First, I know there is often a significant difference between believing you and believing the answer you have given me. That leads me to the second benefit of your answer, namely, that you both gave me the same answer and at least I do not have to make a decision for one of you on the basis of this point."

Chameleon responded in candid humility, "I thank you, not only for your wisdom, but especially for your honesty. Not many people are so forthright with me. Once they learn about me, you know, who I am and what I am like, they use and abuse me. I who attempt to become all things to all people, have endured awful scorn and indescribable suffering. Even in the past, when I have opened myself to someone, as I have to you this night, so that I am quite vulnerable, well, it is at just such times when the sword not only pierces my soul, but is turned by some who delight in the pain of others. Your simple, honest answer of *I don't know*, is the response of either a good friend or a person with a heart of stone. I am not able to look into your heart and see what is there. I only hope and pray that you are not deceiving me with words I want to hear."

Finally, I understood Chameleon, and for the first time, I felt comfortable with him. Now remorse arose for the way I had treated him when he stood in the shadow of the tree. My uncaring query about not tolerating intolerance was spoken with pompous spite. I experienced guilt over my thoughtless words and with it, an immediate apprehension that such shame and sorrow caused me to side with Chameleon.

Tetra Graham roared, "What a sickening, slovenly, shabby, sloppy display of putrid drivel!"

Tetra Graham's volume and intensity shocked me, as did my reaction of agreement. He caught me on the pendulum swing toward Chameleon and took advantage of my movement, almost to the point of driving me to him. I recoiled at the possibility of agreeing with, or being forced to either of their positions.

"Stop! You two must stop. You tell me I am at the point of decision and must go either the way of the rational head or the way of the romantic heart. But there is another way and I will consider it. There is another choice, isn't there?"

They remained silent.

"Let's assume that I accept neither of your arguments and that I refuse to be guided by the mind or influenced by the emotions. In doing so I would reject both of you and both your ways of death. It is the way that denies the objective standard of truth while ignoring any and all personal feelings. This might mean the confession of chaos within and the acceptance of anarchy in the world. However, Tetra Graham and Chameleon, I don't think and I don't really feel that this is a good choice for me. What do you think and feel?"

Chameleon quickly answered, "This is your choice and I feel that you arc the only one to decide. Personally, I like this way because you do have free will and you are exercising it. I say, 'Go for it.' "

After a moment of silence that naturally forced the next reply, Tetra Graham spoke. "You have just received the counsel to try it because you have a choice. I tell you to try it because you have no choice. I think this way because you always opt for life. You always have. You did yesterday and you will tomorrow. You may reject both head and heart, but in the present you opt for life. I have attempted to convince you of the objective reality by using your head, but you were not willing. Now, in order to understand that there is a standard apart from you, you must experience it. Therefore, I also say, 'Go for it.' "

This caught me by surprise for, while I had succeeded in avoiding a commitment to either of them and their respective ways, they were now making the same recommendation, though not for the same reason.

"Nope. Sorry. Rejecting the reality of the head as well as the feelings of the heart is a way of death. It's like," I hesitated as I replied, "it's like being blindfolded and walking in a blizzard."

Immediately Tetra Graham said, "The reality is that there was a blizzard yesterday and you blindly walked about this mountainside."

"What did you feel?"

"What did you think?"

"To clarify what is ahead for you tomorrow, you must reject both the thoughts of your head and the emotions of your heart today."

"I agree. Do it."

"No, that's just not a good idea. But I have enjoyed the thought and the feeling that you two are in agreement with one another."

An approving snicker from one side of the cave preceded an immediate snarl from the other.

"No, you haven't convinced me yet, or rather, I haven't convinced myself. There is another way to go. Instead of rejecting both the rational and the romantic, I will accept both. This way I am able, using my mind to pick and choose what I feel is meet, right and salutary. I have two confessions of life and I will live it by picking and choosing. It is not wise to go against the objective standard or one's conscience. Here I stand. I can do no more. Yet, there really is something not quite right about this. What do you think and feel?"

"I think it is good," said Tetra Graham, "but it falls short. You are not the standard. The laws are outside of you."

Chameleon spoke, "I like this vacillating and of course prefer the picking and choosing that comes with this way of life. You should pursue this way."

"So Chameleon encourages me in this way and Tetra Graham counsels against it?"

Tetra Graham answered, "No. I actually think you should try this, and for the same reason as before. You will learn about the external standard by experience in the world, not by lessons in the classroom."

"Wonderful, that's twice now that you are of one mind and heart," I said with mild sarcasm. "Your agreement with one another reminds me of the ancient declaration, *And Herod and Pilate became friends with each other that very day, for before this they had been at enmity with one another.*"

A litany of snarl and snicker followed.

"Having two confessions and vacillating is also a way of death. I must confess to you two that I am not omniscient and if I make myself the standard, I am only fooling myself. To follow your advice and counsel in this way would be like fooling around in the deadly game of Russian Roulette. Would you have me engage in that? Is that the advice, counsel and recommendation that you would give to me?"

I waited until they answered.

"I think you are beginning to understand."

"Please, say some more. I want to hear you and I do feel your pain."

"Is that it? Is that all you are able to say?"

They waited until I answered.

"Russian Roulette! The objective truth is the bullet in one chamber, the hammer cocked and the laws of nature in effect. The cylinder is spun. I hold the gun to my head. What is my feeling about pulling the trigger? Do I feel that the gun won't fire? Do I think that it will? What do I believe and what do I feel? I could go ahead and spin it again. It wouldn't make any difference. It would not matter if I spin it a million times. The objective truth is always outside of me and, at the same time, I am not omniscient. This is a way of death and I will not walk that way."

I waited.

"I agree with you," said Tetra Graham. "Since you have invoked the old writ, I am reminded of the ancient proverb, *There is a way which seems right to a man, but its end is the way to death.*"

"I also agree," said Chameleon. "Since-"

I interrupted him, "Wait! Who are you talking about? With whom do you agree?"

He replied, "Fortunately, I am pleased to tell you that I agree with both of you. However, my friend, if you decide to play the game, you must pull the trigger. Up to that point you have a choice; after that moment you no longer have a choice. So I am against this way because, though you pick and choose, you have no choice. So I say to you that which was placed before the people long ago. *Choose this day whom you will serve.*"

"And I must choose one of you?"

"You must," came a terse reply from one side of the cave.

"Please choose," sounded softly from the other side.

"Perhaps there is another way."

They did not speak.

"Is not the Standard Maker also the Law Fulfiller?"

Silence.

119

"Is not the Commandment Giver also the Burden-Bearer?"
"He knows."
"Is not the Almighty Court also the Mercy Seat?"
Silence.
"Is not the Omniscient Judge also the Defense Attorney?"
"He does know."
"Is not the Eternal Word also the Sin-Bearer?"
Silence.
"Isn't the LORD God Almighty also the Risen Redeemer?"
"He knows."
"Yes."
"It is beyond him."
"Yes, but he must still choose."
"He knows the truth."
"He must make a decision."

"You know, I have never understood exactly what you are talking about. What do you mean when you say *decision*? It is all beyond me."

"That this is all beyond you does not surprise me. But listen carefully to me."

They began speaking to one another and neglecting me.

"He must accept it in his heart. He must make a decision."

"So this decision is something that man does for God? It's man's work?"

"Yes. That is only reasonable, isn't it? You do understand, don't you?"

"God starts the work in the man and the man finishes it?"
"Yes."

"How about man starting the work and God finishing it?"

"That's okay too. In other words, it is a choice and thus it is acceptable ... just as long as man has some part in saving and justifying himself."

"All of this is beyond him."

"Look, it doesn't matter as long as he's got faith."

"Idiot! It does matter. Faith is nothing."

"Well, just what in the world would you have him do?"

"You blithering fool! He must simply and only and just acknowledge the basic doctrines."

"And?"

I tried to interject myself, "Wait. Stop."

They continued to ignore me.

"And nothing! Why can't I get it into your thick skull, you bonehead? Man only needs to possess the promise, to secure the standard, to put his back to the burden, to shove his shoulder to the law. Once done it doesn't matter if he puts it in a tin can and buries it in the ground. He knows where it's at and is always able to go back to it. It's orthodoxy in a bottle. Take when needed."

"I disagree with you. Faith is the key, the only key. He has to have faith. You know, don't you, that it doesn't really matter what he believes as long as he is sincere."

"You are sickening!"

I tried to speak again. Both of them ignored me.

"He must have a choice and he must choose between you and me."

"It's not like we haven't had this discussion and debate before, you slithering, simpering, anemic, atrophic, wonky, whining, recalcitrant creeper! You maudlin, moronic, morose mugwump! You-"

"Enough, Tetra Graham! I am a man of truth and I will not deceive Chameleon or you. If I have, then I apologize, but enough of your heartless attacks."

"Listen to yourself! You claim to be a man of the truth and yet you are siding with someone who will not acknowledge there is such a thing. Truth to him is whatever you want, feel, desire, wish, hope or will. Why don't you go jump off a cliff? Or have you forgotten?"

"You surprise me, Tetra. I thought you would take me to a pinnacle, show me all the kingdoms of the world and invite me to throw myself down."

121

At this Tetra Graham evoked a sustained guttural from deep within.

"Ommmmmm."

The low tone continued for nearly a minute. I felt a distant vibration, a subtle quaking at the roots of the mountain. The intensity increased and the cutting loose of massive boulders could be heard through the solid rock. Panic ensued as my hands braced against the walls of the cave.

The voice of Chameleon sounded at my left, "Enough! Tetra Graham, tell this man how you spell and pronounce your name."

"No," came the hardened reply to my right.

"Why? He must choose, and in order to do so, he must have the objective truth."

Chameleon's voice turned to me, "He does not spell his name *G-r-a-h-a-m*. It is not pronounced *Graham* either."

I joined the attack. "Listen Tetra, if you have any hopes of my choosing your side, then I better hear some letters and a pronunciation. You are out of time. My decision is forthcoming."

"We are waiting," pressed Chameleon.

All Chameleon and I heard was an uneven, hissing sound as if spittle was being forced through clenched teeth. As the hissing sound continued, Chameleon turned to me and spoke.

"Well, my friend, it appears as if we are in this together, doesn't it? I don't feel comfortable here in his presence. Do you? Perhaps, my friend, we ought to leave."

Before I could utter a syllable in response, someone else stood at the mouth of the cave. He disrupted the discussion and intervened, delaying my decision. A scrambling sound came from the two in the cave with me. I could not identify who moved or who was at the entrance. I saw nothing. Confusion and cacophony reigned momentarily. Someone pushed me aside and the blanket covered my face and swirled about my neck. As I disentangled myself and threw the blanket aside, a shriek filled the cave. One of the two who had been with me was now gone.

The first light before dawn reflected off the snow to give the outline of someone looking in at us. The casting of the shadow revealed only the outline of his upper torso. He spoke as one having authority, "The LORD rebuke you, evil one. The LORD Who has snatched this one from the lake of fire rebuke you."

There was complete silence once more. The figure at the door vanished.

I shouted, "Gabby! Wait, Gabby. Come back."

Silence.

I spoke, "Chameleon. Answer me. Chameleon."

Silence.

I whispered, "Tetra Graham?"

Silence.

CHAPTER 10

WHILE IT WAS STILL DARK

Except for me and my breathing, the cave remained empty and silent. With only the promise of a new day's light in the sky, I determined to leave this inhospitable place hewn out of crude rock. The pre-dawn light reflected off the snow outside and allowed me to make an inspection of the room and its contents. The blanket covered most of the floor to my left. The pack had been cast against the right wall. The small cloth remained neatly folded and in the place where my head had rested during the night.

I emptied the pack and inventoried my food supply. My stash consisted of one biscuit, a small packet of dried apples, another handful of dried cherries, banana chips and several rhubarb stalks. I poked my head out the hole in the stone wall and conducted a quick inspection of the world immediately outside the cave. The spring storm had passed and deep blue spanned the sky to the south. Nearly a foot of fresh snow blanketed the rock floor outside the cave entrance. Convinced I would be able to make Gabby's camp by early afternoon, I ate the biscuit, apples, chips and cherries. The water from the canteen further refreshed me and I resolved to drink only half the remaining water. Within ten minutes I had prepared the pack. I put the coat, hat and gloves on and emerged from the cave entrance.

During the night, the snow on the floor of the cleft had drifted as the wind swirled through the rock corridor. The open end of the cleft dropped to the narrow path where I had been blinded by the wind. On the downhill side of this ledge the slope dropped at a steep decline. A step off the path in the snowstorm would have sent me tumbling into a deep crevasse. My heart rate increased as I shed the pack and carefully negotiated my way to the ledge and the snow-covered path. With the pack in place once again, the journey to camp began as the day dawned.

During the storm, the snow also drifted at the base of the sentinel. The entire mountainside had received a blanket of fresh snow. Only the dark rock outcroppings on the downhill side gave any contrast to the white overlay. I guessed the snowfall to be a foot or more, possibly eighteen inches. The air had warmed, possibly to forty degrees. A spring chinook blew across the mountain and began melting the snow at a rapid rate. The top inch of snow squished under my feet as I stepped along. Ahead of me the mountainside glistened with a milky dullness.

The journey eastward across the snowfield and the risen sun directly ahead produced a blinding light, a brilliance doubled by the reflecting snow. The sun reflected off my cheeks. I tied the small cloth around my head and face in order to reduce the lower glare. I tilted the bill of my hat to diminish the upper glare. Even with slits where my eyes peeked out and with the shaded cover above and below them, the light blinded me. At least the wind at my back did not add to the irritation of my stinging eyes.

The temperature rose, the wind maintained its strength and the snow continued to melt. The snowfield ahead changed from a pristine white to a glistening opaque. Within an hour the slush approached the top of my boots. Lifting and plodding made the walk long and strenuous. Several times I stopped to check the position of the sentinel at my back and was awestruck as the early morning light displayed the majestic beauty of the cold rock. The wind prevented a prolonged view since it further dried my painful eyes. Soon the slop soaked my pants to the knees and, in the process, seeped into my boots.

After two hours I approached the eastern edge of the old snowfield. The snow that had fallen on the bare ground disappeared through sublimation into the air and infiltration into the granular soil. I estimated the temperature to be approaching sixty degrees. The melt in such locations increased as wind and sun combined to remove the snow from the landscape. While the sun no longer shone directly in my eyes and the glare off the opaque slush became insignificant, the damage had been done to my eyes and it hurt to open them. I was sweating due to the exertion of the trek and the warm winds. Earlier I had unbuttoned Gabby's thick coat. Now I removed it and stuffed it in the pack. My back chilled and I shivered as the wind evaporated the sweat in my newly exposed shirt.

By the time I traversed the old snowfield, no trace of the newly fallen snow remained. The coarse, gritty soil that lodged between the larger rocks became saturated with the seeping water. Despite the waterlogged boots, walking was easier on the solid ground. The warm wind continued as I approached the ravine.

I sensed a faint, deep rumbling and was not entirely certain whether the sensation came by hearing or feeling. I stood still and held my breath in an attempt to discern the direction and derivation of the rumble. Depth. The deep places of the earth. These are what I sensed. As I continued my hike to the point where the descent to the south could commence, I approached the ravine. The roaring of the deep increased in length, breadth and volume. Throughout the constant rumblings, low frequency vibrations suddenly strengthened in magnitude and decreased almost as quickly. Ten feet from the ravine I viewed an unrelenting flood and heard the sound of a rushing river. It took on an existence and will of its own. Below the surface, the irresistible force cast massive boulders into one another. The mammoth grinding produced sounds that reverberated within me, that is, within my lungs. Millions of tons of rock, grit, sand and water scoured, deepened and widened the ravine as gravity pulled the recently formed river down the mountainside. Loosened sides of the crevasse slid into the water and joined the juggernaut.

Awestruck at the sound and frightened at the possibility of the ground sloughing beneath my feet, I retreated to a safe distance, shed the pack and sat down. I would not repeat the mistake committed by the hound yesterday. I stayed far from the edge. I closed my eyes in relief, now no longer having to receive and process visual information. With peaceful clarity, my body felt and heard the sounds of water, stone and boulder. The wind gradually ceased and I reclined on a recessed spot of ground. The air became still and calm. I relaxed.

Half the water in the canteen nearly satisfied my thirst. Eye strain, the night in the cave and the mountain travels of the last few days caused a weariness to settle on and overcome me. Once more my shoulders felt the place where the pack straps had borne down on them. With my legs stretched, I leaned against the pack, using it as a pillow. The cap covered my face as the midday sun seeped through clothing and into flesh and bones. Weariness covered me like a pall. I intended to permit myself a single moment to relax completely. A moment extended to hours as I slept in the warm sunshine.

I woke with a start and muttered chastisements on myself for being slothful and stupid. The sun had curled to the west and three or four hours remained before sunset. I rose to begin the descent, determining to make camp before that time. With the pack in place, I began the hike at an increased pace. The forced march required mental discipline and physical stamina. The green patch would be kept to the right, the invisible line of the mysterious cliff to the left. I made good time through the areas of small rock and glacial castings. One slip resulted in a fall that tore a pant leg, scraped a knee and put a knot on the opposite elbow. Fields of larger rocks slowed my pace. A fall in one of these areas could inflict a serious injury or result in a life-threatening situation.

Every quick step on the way down led to a quicker next one and required the use of my legs to slow down. The front of my thighs burned with the strain. Minutes before sunset I went through the valley of the shadows and over the small ridge at Gabby's camp. Sudden disappointment engulfed me. The once

placid stream had transformed into a formidable river. The swift, roaring, raging torrent prevented my attempt at crossing.

The woman stood on the other side shaking her hands in frustration. Her actions appeared peculiar. She beckoned. She pleaded. Although too far away to see her clearly in the dimming light, she seemed frightened and distraught. I panicked. The unanswerable questions came rapidly to me, "How long would it take this river to subside? Will they be safe alone this night? Where were Chameleon and Tetra Graham? Would we be able to leave together in the morning? Was there a place downstream where they could cross to me?"

I shouted to her, "Go back to the shelter."

The noise from the stream kept her from hearing me. She cried and yelled, but I could neither hear her voice nor read her lips. Though aware of the futility, I made another attempt,

"Where is the boy?" She did not understand me. Frustrated, she covered her face with her hands and slumped to the ground. No doubt, she wanted to spend the last night of our camping trip together. I imagined the same questions I asked myself were going through her mind. The boy remained out of sight. Evidently mindful of the treacherous current, the woman wisely kept the boy in the stable and away from these dangerous waters. I could do nothing to reassure or comfort her. A gulf of noise kept us from communicating. A chasm of liquid chaos separated us. We could only look at one another in a day growing dim. I stood gazing at her for long, frustrating minutes. She did not move, but continued to rest her head on her knees.

Having to stand at a distance when a loved one is in such distress or in sickness, anxiety, pain or facing death is awful. To behold such a one as this, such a one who needs comfort and consolation, and to be able to give none, is one of the most agonizing and helpless positions there is. When simply reaching out a hand to help is impossible, the forced reaction is to do nothing or to walk away. The woman did the former; I did the latter. Both of us cried out to God.

Darkness descended on both the camp and my spirit. Frustrated, anxious, frightened, angry, worried and forlorn I resigned myself to the objective reality of the torrent and though I willed it not to be, it remained. Simply and absolutely I could do nothing to go to the woman and the boy that night. I willed to be with them but I could not do it. Her head sank deeper to her chest as she slumped to her knees. Her still figure slowly faded from my gaze amidst the shadows. Soon she would be gone, disappearing from my sight and in a few fleeting minutes I would be left with only a memory of what she looked like in the night, an image of her in distress and anguish. From her perspective, I began vanishing as well. From what I could determine, she never gazed in my direction. With darkness having conquered the day, I could do nothing but walk away from the deadly rush of water. I knew things would be better in the morning light of a new day and assuaged myself with that hope.

Gabby puttered around his campsite. He gave the impression of being in somber thought, saying nothing as he warmed a saucepan of milk over a few embers. Most of the coals had lost their glow as the fire slowly died. This low fire would only keep the milk from cooling.

I almost expected to hear him say, "It does you no good if you remain distant." That's a great saying if someone has the capability of responding to a cup of warm milk or a glass of cold water. But tonight, when I needed to be reunited with the woman and the boy, I could only remain distant. A great gulf separated us. How long would the separation be?

Gabby gave me a cup of milk.

"Thanks, Gabby."

No reply.

I sipped the warm milk and the surface scum stuck to my top lip. A sudden anxiety overwhelmed me and I cast a glance into the night shadows beyond the camp. Had the woman moved from her treacherous spot and gone into the shelter with the boy? The fire here provided light and warmth. Did they have the same in the shelter? A simple cup of warm milk rested in my hand. Did they have anything to eat or drink over there? I wept silently, my tears falling to and being absorbed in the already saturated earth.

In sorrow and frustration, I lifted my head and stared once more in the direction of the woman and the boy. I willed to see them with my eyes but only saw them in my mind. They had not received much attention from me this weekend. I promised the Almighty and myself that things would be different with the woman and the boy. From this moment on, the fruits worthy of repentance began. Maybe Gabby had been right about the importance of this weekend on the mountain. Perhaps I needed this dividing river to understand the importance of the others. If I required an interruption in my life for these good purposes, then God must have let all this happen to draw me closer to Him and ultimately to them.

Though the longing of my heart to be reunited with my family did not cease, peace permeated my soul as a long draught of the milk passed down my throat and warmed my stomach. Confession to God, even if only in one's mind, unloaded a heavy burden and the absolution of His Word heard so often in the past satisfied my spirit. Understanding that the LORD guided and guarded the woman and the boy, I let them go into His hands and care for the night. I comforted myself that flash floods disappear as quickly as they arrive. The dawning of a new day would remove the rift between us.

With the cup drained, I desired to sleep. It was not so much that my weariness created this yearning, but that I especially wanted the night to be gone quickly. Sleep takes away the conscious knowledge of life's present troubles. For those suffering the tragic loss of a loved one, sleep gives a period of respite. For me, sleep this night would make the time pass without notice. When there is hope for the coming day, then one can endure the darkness of earth's one evening. The longing for the night to be over rises and with such a resurrection, hope is born. I resolved to be up early tomorrow morning. They must not be permitted to come to me. Indeed not, I must go to them.

Gabby interrupted my thoughts.

"You need solid food."

"No, Gabby, I don't think so. This milk is going to be enough. It is all the nourishment needed tonight. I want to sleep."

"Not physical food," Gabby replied, "but spiritual. The need you have is to go beyond spiritual milk and to chew on some solid food. The journey you are on is not one that can be made only with milk. Even with solid food, your particular trek may be too much for you."

"Gabby, you make it sound as if it has already begun and that you don't know how it will end. Is that true?"

"That is correct," he responded, "in both cases. Your great ordeal commenced a few hours ago and only God knows if you will endure. Please, you must continue beginning. I am here to help you answer your questions."

I had no desire to wrestle with words at this hour. Frustrated and searching for a question, I asked, "Why is it just hot milk tonight and not hot cocoa."

"Please, do not be silly," he implored.

Though I was becoming tired and not especially in the mood for discussion, I continued half-heartedly, "It seems like a good question. Please answer it."

Gabby sighed and began, "You should know the answer. The other night you were told that hot cocoa helps you to sleep and promotes night visions. On that night you needed to dream so you had hot cocoa. Tonight you drink hot milk because you need sleep and rest for the time that has arrived. Tomorrow there will be bread and wine. Now, please, a question with substance."

The gravity of his speech impressed me. However, there was nowhere to begin. I felt pressured as I had the previous night. The same issue came to mind and without sincere commitment or careful discernment, I asked, "Gabby, is God responsible for evil?"

His eyes narrowed in focus and sparkled in keen interest. "Now you have asked a question. Ask me the very same question using different words."

Startled, I responded, "To be honest with you, Gabby, you surprise me. I expected an immediate *no* for an answer. Is it at all possible that there is a case in which *yes* might be your response?"

"You need to be specific with your query so the response is understood. Yours is a most important question. However, the sense of it must be discerned. The meanings of a word are critical. Be careful how you ask."

"Maybe it wasn't a good question after all. Let me withdraw it and think of another."

Gabby flashed back, "No! The question is especially important to you this night. But it must be stated and understood with clarity and precision before it is addressed."

"Look, Gabby, I simply asked if God was the author of evil."

"No, you did not" he spoke with a quick, attacking firmness, "you asked, *Is God responsible for evil?* That is a different question than, *Is God the author of evil?* The answer to the latter is a certain *no.* God did not create evil. Evil can not find its origin in God."

He was pushing me to go further and I continued, "Is evil a substance?"

"No."

"Well, since evil has no being of itself, it must be conjured, appropriated or acquired by one that exists. Then the revision put forth is this, *Did God create the evil one?* Please, Gabby, give a simple *yes* or *no* as your answer."

"Either of those answers would be incomplete and give false impressions. An adequate reply is that God is the Creator of that one who later willed and worked departure from God. That one suffered, and is suffering the consequences of having God's holiness and goodness removed. The one who later became the evil one was originally part of God's good creation. That one, like other fallen messengers who did not keep their proper place, has fallen so far and so completely that it is self-obsessed, venomous, violent and vitriolic."

After a few minutes, I asked, "How might I further clarify my question so you may respond? .... Is God responsible for the evil one?"

"The word *responsible* is too slippery here. The word may be used in such a way that it makes God guilty of sin because He is the blame or cause of the works of the evil one in the world. Or, the word is used to give a picture of the evil one going to and fro on the earth, walking back and forth on it, and doing evil. Then God, like some befuddled grandpa who feels compelled to pick up the pieces, scurries here and there attempting to undo all these things."

I said, "Both of those are obviously answered with a *no*. In what sense is the word used whereby there is a *yes* answer?"

Gabby heightened as he inhaled. Then he spoke, "Now you have come upon the question!"

"Do you have the answer?"

"No, no one is able to know it completely. However, if it is considered with care and received as intended then perhaps we are able to approach a certain understanding. God is good. God is everywhere except where He has willed not to be. Wherever God is not, there is the evil one's place or the achievements of the same. However, there is more. God has permitted an overlap, allowing the evil one to be in a place where God is. This world is an example of such a place. The Author of good and the forces of the evil one are here and that is why it is so difficult for the descendants of Adam and Eve. In fact, had God not specially revealed Himself in this world, there would be no point of reference for a gracious God, no basis for the merciful God to be known. All would have been only under the justice of God. None of this would ever be known among you. Since God has revealed Himself and told you what His good and gracious will is, and has shown you that will at Sinai and Golgotha, there is a point of reference which usually gives an indication what is of God and what is not. Consequently, from your point of view, God is responsible for having made manifest both the evil one as well as its deeds among you, while at the same time, we must maintain that God is not responsible for evil."

"Gabby, give me something to help, an example or analogy."

"Alright. Look into the stand of trees to the west. Tell me about the shadows of those trees."

"That's not possible for me. I am not even able to see the trees in this darkness, let alone the shadows. Right now, I could not prove to you that there even is a stand of trees over there. How is it possible to identify shadows when everything is in darkness?"

"Exactly. In order to expose those dark places, a great light would need to shine and reveal the shadows that lurk and lengthen behind the visible things of this world. The evil one and all associated works and ways are the shadows skulking in the dark. God, Who is Light, makes them known. God is responsible for those shadows being manifested."

With a point in mind I asked, "May I attempt to describe another comparison?"

"Please do."

"Let's try the truth. God has revealed the truth to us. Whatever is not the truth is a lie, a false teaching, a false doctrine. However, in our blinded state in this fallen world, we would not know what lies, untruths or false doctrines were had we not had the truth revealed to us by God, Who has done so by nature and by His Word. So we would not be wrong in maintaining that the truth is responsible for all the false teachings in the world that have followed. However we would never hold the truth guilty because of all the lies it exposes."

Gabby confessed, "This is most certainly true. The same could be said of the Bible. God has given you the Bible and it means what God intends it to mean, nothing more, nothing less. He is the author and each word, phrase and sentence has one intended meaning, namely, the meaning God had when He caused it to be written. However, many ungodly beliefs and practices have come about because the Scriptures have been interpreted erroneously and applied incorrectly. Therefore, the Word of God is responsible for all the malicious teachings and activities which are derivations from Holy Writ and have gone forth in God's Name. Still, you would not hold either God or the Bible guilty."

"Gabby, these are good examples and I do understand what you are saying. But they only concern themselves with what we are able to identify as the works of the evil one or the existence of truth and lie. A few minutes ago you said that the way God reveals Himself is usually an indication, but not always. Why? Why can't we be sure?"

"Sometimes, from your perspective, it is impossible to tell who is doing what. For one thing, the evil one often appears as an angel of light. The evil one is often quite radiant and pleasing to the eye, the beautiful devil. So things may not be as they appear. For another, God often does or permits things that are contrary to what you might want or expect. In fact, the greatest revelation of God's love was when it met His wrath in the ugliness of an execution. Darkness overshadowed the sun for three hours at midday. And when it was finished, there hardly appeared any sort of victory by God or for Him. But by that death came life. So once again, things were not as they seemed."

"But what of the continued existence of the evil one? How do God and the evil one co-exist? Again, give me a picture."

"Fine, but remember the example has its points of comparison as well as points where it may not hold true. Also, it is here that we are journeying very close to the edge. We must be ready and willing to stop peering into the unrevealed, to step back and to walk away without answers. The hidden things belong to the LORD God. What belongs to you is what He has revealed to you. He has not revealed all things to you."

I told him I understood and asked him to continue with an example.

Gabby nodded and replied, "Consider the possibility that God is this mountain and whatever is not God is not mountain. So, the cave you were in last night was either mountain or not mountain."

He waited. Obviously, a reply was expected. Attempting to be as discerning as possible, I offered, "In the most strict, technical sense, the cave is not mountain."

"Correct."

"So, while God is the mountain, the cave is a creation."

"Right again. However, the cave only has its being and meaning because of the mountain. It is defined by the existence of the mountain. The mountain determines the cave's dimensions, shape and limits, as well as what may or may not be in the cave. The cave is as real as the mountain, but the cave's reality and limits are based upon the existence of the mountain."

I continued to build on the example.

"What about me? I am neither the cave nor the mountain."

He replied, "You occupy a certain place for a limited time in the cave."

"It was in that cave I escaped certain death. Without the cave I would have been lost. The cave saved me and protected me."

He replied, "No, the mountain did. But here is also where the analogy begins to break down."

This discussion strained me. My mind became weary and cluttered. Mentally I juggled too many examples and thoughts.

"Gabby, this all sounds very theoretical. There really does not seem to be much practical application in this."

He looked intently at me and replied, "Our discussions are most practical for you. They are as practical as the guidance and protection you received yesterday and last night. They are as practical as what you will need in the future."

I closed my eyes momentarily and sighed, "Okay. But give me another example."

"You have not exhausted the implications and lessons from the ones already given. There are additional points to compare and thoughts to consider."

"I know. I'll think further on these later. Give me another example, Gabby."

"Imagine that an accident takes place when a suspension bridge gives way and a woman is killed in the fall. God is said to be guilty because it was His will that she died when the trail bridge collapsed."

"Well, wasn't it His will?"

"Think for a minute and answer these questions in your own mind. Was it the will of God that the structural engineer made a mistake in the calculations? Was it truly the will of God that the computer programmer hit the wrong key when entering design load data? Was it really the will of God that the manufacturer of the support bracing cut corners by using a lower grade of lumber? Was it His will that the building contractor did not torque the nuts and bolts to the required specifications? These things and fifty others were not the will of God. But He does get blamed for all of this and more."

I confessed, "Your example demonstrates the point according to the way you describe the scenario. But, how do you respond to a natural disaster? What's a good example? Let's say that ... well okay, let's say the woman, rather than falling to her death when a man-made bridge collapses, drowns when a flash flood sweeps her away."

Gabby spoke with immediate determination, "Do not speak of this. Give me some other example."

"What? Uhhh. Okay. Uhhh. Say a teenage girl is hiking just below the sentinel when an earthquake dislodges some boulders above her. They fall on her and kill her. No one else had any part in this natural disaster. What can be said of God and His will?"

"There are several issues to address here. Let me summarize them and then we can go into some details. First, there is nothing natural about such tragic events. Death is neither natural nor God's original intent for anyone. Second, there are differences between God's will, foreknowledge and providence. And third, there is the alien work of God, a strange work of His. Fourth, there is His antecedent and consequent-"

"Hey Gabby, I'm sorry to interrupt, but my body aches, my eyes burn and my mind is getting weary. I'm not sure how long I will be able to concentrate tonight. Perhaps we will speak of these things tomorrow."

He replied, "We will not speak of these things again."

"We might."

Ignoring my rebuttal, he said, "There will be no more time for us other than tonight."

"Well," I muttered, "it looks like I made the right choice anyway."

"That would be true if God's choosing or election before the foundation of the world were based upon your decision in time. That is not the situation. You can not, by your own reason or strength believe in Jesus Christ or come to Him. The Holy Spirit has called you by the Gospel and given you the gift of faith to trust this Good News. Part of the Gospel is that He chose you, that He made a decision for you."

"Enough! Gabby, you turn everything around, as if I have gotten it all backwards. Tomorrow, okay?"

He repeated, "There will be no more time for us other than tonight."

"Sorry Gabby. I have to sleep. As soon as I see the risen sun, I want to go across and be with the woman and the boy."

139

In a neutral, almost disappointed or disgusted voice, he replied, "A sleeping bag is ready for you in the tent."

"Thanks."

No reply.

I placed my wet, smelly boots and socks near the dying fire. Gingerly I moved to the tent on clammy, tender feet. My cold feet and the short walk to the tent cleared my mind. After getting into bed for the night I stared through the tent opening. In the darkness of the silent night, I wondered and I asked.

"Gabby, you are not the mountain, are you?"

"I am not the mountain."

"God is the mountain?"

"Yes."

"Did the mountain become a cave?"

"No, the mountain became man."

"Was that Man still the mountain?"

"Yes."

"Did He come to live in this world?"

"Yes."

"Why?"

"You know why."

"To suffer the hellish onslaught of the minions of the evil one and to endure the holy wrath of God against sin as He atoned for the transgressions of all people of all times?"

"Yes."

"He shed His holy blood and gave His innocent life for the world?"

"Yes."

"And they buried Him?"

"It was more like they put Him in a cave and rolled a death stone over its entrance."

"Then He rose from the dead and left the cave?"

"Yes."

"Was He in the cave with me last night?"

"He was, but not in the same way you were in the cave."

"What do you mean?"

"You have a comprehensible, corporeal mode of presence. He is not limited to that mode of presence and was not there in that manner."

"Comprehensible, corporeal mode of presence?"

"You walk bodily on this earth and vacate or occupy a certain space according to your physical dimensions."

"Are there other modes of presence that He has?"

"Yes."

"But He was not in the cave in His comprehensible, corporeal mode of presence last night?"

"Correct."

"Maybe tomorrow we will discuss the other ways that He is able to be present."

"No. Other than this evening, there will be no time for you and me to discuss these matters."

Neither of us spoke for a few moments.

"Gabby, is that mountain still man?"

"Yes, begotten from eternity, born in time, always is."

I yawned and thought before speaking.

"When we were hiking up the mountain you said there were four reasons why you were there. One was to talk with me. Another was to carry the pack part of the way. The third was to show me the rock where the cave was. What was the fourth?"

Pausing for a moment, he answered, "I am a messenger. The time to call the contender drew near."

"Who is the contender?"

"The contender is also a messenger."

"Was the contender the one outside the cave who stopped the proceedings?"

"Yes."

"What was he contending for?"

"For you."

"With whom was he contending?"

"The evil one."

141

"When?"

"Generally, throughout your life, but especially this weekend and most particularly last night when you were in the cave with the evil one."

"The evil one? But there were two in the cave with me."

"No, only one. There was never more than one."

"Never more than one?"

"Correct."

I thought over the events of the last days, attempting not to pass over the details, however this quickly became futile since physical weariness and mental fatigue overwhelmed me. These things would be considered in the alertness and clarity of a new day. Top and bottom lids slid together. Perhaps one last question could be answered.

In the dark quiet of the last moments of consciousness, I mumbled from my bed, "Messenger, you said in these woods and among those who live on the mountain, Gabby is your name. Who are you? What is your given name?"

A continued moment of silence passed. It didn't really matter. I snuggled deeper into the sleeping bag. But in that time when one is neither asleep nor awake, I believe, I'm not certain but I think, I believe, I heard his reply whispered softly in my ear.

"Gabriel."

CHAPTER 11

A LITTLE ONE'S EIGHTH DAY

There was morning. The dawn of a new day arrived as it always had, save that one exception, since the LORD God said *Let there be* and there was evening and there was morning, one day.

The man experienced a fitful sleep that night and slept beyond the beginning of the day. As had been on a thousand days and more, the old man remained in his bed with the restraint rail up and in place. The bed was located in the far left corner of the room. The window treatment consisted of a top border of faded green cotton. The frayed fringe of the border had lost its color from years of service in the sun. Even the slow-flowing glass showed signs of age. Scratches from inside cleaning and blowing grit on the outside reduced the clarity to that of obscure glass. The window at his back allowed the sunlight by day and the moonbeams by night to smite the old man.

Except for a clock above the head of his bed, the walls were bare. The clock clicked off the seconds of time for anyone who came into the room, not for the man in the bed. Anyone looking at the timepiece from the old man's position would have had to tilt his head far back and possess the ability to read the clock upside down. Besides, the timepiece could not have been of any benefit to the old man because the tunneling of his light narrowed to the point where he had lost his eyesight years earlier.

On the other side of the room, a radio had been placed on a stand. The scratchy-sounding radio with the faded maroon case remained on for the benefit of others who came into the room. Those who entered his room and preferred to listen to something else changed the station. The radio did not benefit the old man. He had lost his hearing a decade earlier. A vase, beside the radio and somewhat centered on a dingy, white-laced doily, contained three plastic flowers. The two daffodils had been purged of color and the red tulip was now an anemic pink.

The old man, with his right arm under the side of his head and thumb fixed below his ear, reclined in the bed on his right side. He preferred this side, not because he feared someone suddenly appearing in the window behind him, but because this position put less pressure on his heart. Being on the left side gave him heart pains after a few minutes.

His eyes, long clouded over with cataracts, gazed on objects not in this world. Ears were useless attachments. They only sent a constant feed of silent static to the brain. Taste buds had long ago ceased working. No matter, had they been in service they would have only sensed the bad taste of bland food injected into the back of his mouth with a syringe or the foul flavor of oral abscesses that continuously drained. Long ago, his sense of smell acclimated to the institutional aromas and his personal odors. In order to provide his mind with a sense of being alive, as well as being able to affirm and acknowledge his existence, he would holler and moan. He felt the vibrations within his chest.

From the world's viewpoint, the old man had long been a deficit. His continued life served no apparent purpose. He aged into uselessness. Yelling and shaking occurred when unseen hands and unwanted tending disturbed him. He became a tape-recorder on auto-play. People who walked by his room or tended to him heard the same unconnected rambling over and over and over. He occupied a room at the far end of the special wing. Friends and family visitors seldom came to that section. No matter, the old man had neither. Except for those times when he registered his disapproval for feeding, changing and bathing, the old man communicated with no one in the outside world. At all other times the shell of a man was unresponsive. While he had being and

145

10

occupied a definite space, the world could not reach him. His membership in society had been cancelled by a failure to respond.

His pastor stopped on various occasions, but the old man never knew of his visits. The readings and the prayers, while heard by God, fell on old, deaf ears. Once a year, just before Christmas, usually late on a Sunday afternoon, carolers from various churches came by and sang, though not for very long in the special wing. He never heard the hymns and, while he did confess the Incarnation of the Son of God, he did not know when the Festival of the Nativity was being celebrated.

Still, the old man had not been called home to the LORD. The dark box of the old man's mind was now the world he roamed. His senses no longer relayed external messages and images to him. Thus he resided in an unlit niche of varied memories and thoughts. Prayers were numerous as he thanked and praised God while petitioning for himself and for the others whom he loved. Many of those others, however, were beyond the need for such prayers of deliverance. Learned years ago from caring pastors who fed the people of God with repetition, the rest home resident silently chanted the historic liturgies and sang the hymns of Christendom. Stanzas of one hymn gave way to a petition from the Lord's Prayer that evolved into the middle section of the Pledge of Allegiance to a section of the Agnus Dei. He recalled similar tunes and hummed them as interludes. His thoughts continued throughout his waking hours. Again and again, day after day, over and over, night after night he mentally listened to the Te Deum Laudamus and relived the scenarios of past days and lost opportunities.

Mental discipline was necessary to prevent insanity. Often physical restraints restricted his range of motion. If he had an itch, a bed sore or a headache, he had no way of letting anyone know, and certainly no possibility of caring for himself. Coping with pain became a continual activity; blocking it out an unrealized goal. More times than could be remembered he uttered a silent scream, "out of the depths I cry unto Thee; how long, O LORD, how long?"

Thoughtful diversion was helpful with any of the minor physical pains. The woman had once taught him a number game that could be played in the mind. Pick any number, or if a sentence is "my favorite dog is named Sport," you count out the number of letters in that sentence. She would say, "That is twenty-five letters. Twenty-five is 'two numbers, ten letters' and it counts out to twenty. Twenty is 'one number, six letters' and it counts out to nineteen. Since nineteen is a favorite number, you stop." She reminded her husband that sometimes the game doesn't work so that you get a favorite number. "When that happens," she would say, "you stop the game or pick a new phrase, word, sentence or number." His caregivers often saw his fingers ticking off letters as she had shown him and they thought it was just nervous motion or uncontrolled twitching.

At other times the old man hid from enemy soldiers as he had done so long ago. The soldiers had grown old too. Their weapons were outdated and the ammo had been used in earlier skirmishes with the old man. Hiding always required him to remain motionless under a pile of leaves. Having to hide too long put him to sleep.

Being imprisoned in the mind became dreadfully painful. The worst came when he awoke from a horribly real nightmare and could only open his eyes to the darkness of his mind, and could only open his mind to the darkness of his eyes. Getting bearings, as well as finding out the what and where of reality, was nearly impossible. Thrashing about and yelling only brought his nightmare to intense reality as he discovered the restraints. He had been left to the mercy of gargoyles and ghouls. At moments of such extreme mental anguish and with the frightful suffering which found no relief, the old man would call out for his mother. She never came and he endured. He had no choice. He begged for her to come to him. He trembled while wondering why she had deserted him. In the corridors outside, his pleading scream was heard, "Mommy! Where is my mommy?"

If an instrument were invented to provide a scanned picture of a human soul, the image of the old man's soul would have revealed brutal wounds, severe scars and open sores. The deepest stroke came when the Lion of Judah stretched forth a clawed paw and swiped the boy away. This loss left an open sore on the old man's soul that pained him for more than half a century. Throughout the black universe of his senseless world he still asked, "Why?" Dried-up tear ducts only functioned when his thoughts lingered on the boy. His little one, taken away too young, left an unhealed, open sore on his heart. A life not lived by another is a loss to those who are left to continue. Not only did he have to go on, but he continued without those he loved. There would be no children from the boy and consequently, the old man would weep at the empty spots in photo albums. In earlier days he could occupy time with work or thoughts that chased away the theoretical scenarios. When the years put him in bed, the imaginations of his heart assaulted him without mercy.

In his conscious thoughts and unconscious dreams, children's laughter haunted and mocked him. Sometimes a boy and girl tromped through the woods ahead of the old man. The troop followed mountain trails along the banks of creeks. The trio threw rocks into the water and searched for creatures under stones. The children would run ahead, hide behind fallen trees and jump out when the old man finally caught up and drew close. Several times an older boy would fish with him. The old man exhaled deeply when he remembered that this boy remained the offspring of his imagination. No young lady walked down the aisle in white on her wedding day. She would not wink at the hunched man in the pew near the front; no smiling at the old man whom she called grandfather.

The vision always returned to the younger girl grasping a wilted trillium just below the blossom. This four-year old, dressed in a red flannel shirt that hung out the sides of faded, blue bib overalls, would be running to him. Red locks of hair curled down under her ear lobes or matted against her high forehead. Blue eyes sparkled in excitement and with sheer delight at being able to share some wonderful discovery with the old man. Baby teeth flashed as she giggled and called him to "lookie, see what I got, Gampa." With choked trillium in hand, she ran to him with arms extended and body leaning forward. The old man anticipated her faithful fall into his strong hands. She never made it to his arms, while the tears of disappointment always came to his eyes. He wept for this redheaded girl who never was.

In the bitter irony of things not being the way one wants or expects, the woman died more than a decade earlier. Her pain became so great he wanted to let her go. But letting her go meant a part of him would die with her. After she died, he had pain descending to places deeper than he thought existed within him, and when it got there, it descended farther. He cried and realized that he had never cried before. The open wound on his soul caused by this ungodly slash never healed. Battles with confusion and hatred were fought. A litany of utterances were mentally spoken, "My God, if You are there, answer me, *Why*?" "I did not know pain like this existed." "Though He slay me, yet will I trust in Him." Then he prayed, "Please, oh please, slay me." And from God? Silence. Sleep usually ended these chronic, sobbing struggles amidst the shadows and silence of his world. The old man never recovered from this affliction.

In the last weeks, his thoughts scattered and the length of his meditations shortened. Neither logic, nor liturgical order, nor the proper distinction of justification and sanctification, nor reason any longer dictated the sequence of thoughts. Now the ministry of the Word, the ancient liturgies, the church lectionary, the hymnody of Christendom and the required memory work from his early years served him.

"We praise Thee, O God, we acknowledge Thee to be the LORD ... Create in me a clean heart, O God, and renew a right spirit within me. Cast me not away from Thy presence; and take not Thy Holy Spirit from me .... I cannot, by my own reason or strength, believe in Jesus Christ my Lord or come to Him, but the Holy Ghost has called me by the Gospel .... very God of very God, begotten not made, being of one substance with the Father by Whom all things were made .... for what is man that Thou art mindful of him? .... Our Father, Who art in heaven ... Heaven is my home .... When I thirst He bids me go where the quiet waters flow .... Matthew, Mark, Luke, John .... O God, give us this day our daily bread ... such as food, drink, clothing, shoes, house, home, fields, cattle, money, goods, a pious spouse ... why did You take my wife? ... house and home, wife and children and all my goods, pious children .... why, oh why did You take the boy and leave me here? .... this is My Body given for you .... I am but a stranger here, heaven is my home ... they won't find me in this cave and I am in this cave where no one knows where I am and no one will find me in this cave .... for I know the plans I have for you, says the LORD, plans for welfare and not for evil to give you a future and a hope .... a broken and a contrite heart, O God, Thou wilt not despise .... I am baptized! .... my desire is to depart and be with Christ .... we know that in all things God works for good for those who love Him, who are called according to His purpose .... *pain in my feet* .... the hound, the hound .... I, a poor miserable sinner, confess unto Thee all my sins and iniquities with which I have ever offended Thee and justly deserve Thy temporal and eternal punishment ... to whom shall I go? You have the words of eternal life .... leave me alone whoever you are .... Light of Light, very God of very God, begotten, not made, being of one substance with the Father .... the woman, oh, the woman .... oh my soul praise Him for He is thy Health and Salvation .... in sickness and in health .... 'til death us do part .... I don't have to do my memory work, I get to do it .... Jesus wept .... servant of the Word announce the grace of God unto all of you, and in the stead and by the command of my Lord Jesus Christ, I forgive you all your sins .... if I should die before I wake I pray the LORD my soul to take .... *pain in my knees* .... the LORD make His face to shine upon you and grant you peace .... Now I am eighty-six years old and am about to die. What have you come to ask of me? 'Your benediction,' said the bishop .... when I thirst He bids me go .... there is now, therefore, no condemnation for those who are in Christ Jesus .... Do you have a hole in your head? .... You can't be a mugwump .... Don't let your ears itch .... maid and matron hymn Thy glory .... stay on task .... the highest worship of God is to receive the forgiveness of sins .... LORD, now lettest Thou Thy servant depart in peace, according to Thy Word .... my desire is to depart and be with Christ .... Martha, Martha .... and with you .... Forgive me not according to my unworthiness, but according to Thy loving kindness .... Chameleon .... I baptize you in the Name of the Father and of the Son and of the Holy Ghost .... to Thee all angels cry aloud, the heaven and all the powers therein .... woman, I want to be with you .... all hail the power of Jesus' Name, let angels prostrate fall .... Tetra Graham .... *leg pain* .... get away from me now! .... roads go ever ever on, over rock and under tree, by caves where never sun has shone .... you will be with Me in Paradise .... a mighty fortress is our God .... and as we are strangers and pilgrims on earth, help us by true faith and a godly life to prepare for the world to come .... asleep in Jesus oh, for me, may such a blissful refuge be! .... He maketh me to lie down in green pastures and when I thirst He bids me go .... *my legs are numb* .... Paul, James, Peter .... Lord, be with my brothers .... Holy Ghost with light Divine shine upon this heart of mine, chase the shades of night away, turn the darkness into day .... read, mark, learn and inwardly digest .... April 16, 1947 .... I have redeemed you, I have called you by name, you are Mine .... very good food, Gabby .... watchman, tell us of the night for I know that my Redeemer lives .... is that all there is? .... Joy to the world, the Lord is come, nor thorns infest the ground far as the curse is found .... I feel nothing below my waist ... please, slay me now and let me be, consecrated Lord to Thee .... who from our mother's arms .... shed for you .... what can man do unto me? .... created in Christ Jesus for good works which He prepared beforehand .... I must keep my ears from itching .... praise Father, Son and Holy Ghost, amen ... the Bridegroom lives Who once was dead .... my desire is to depart and be with Christ .... no, not yet? .... this is My Blood .... I repent of my sin .... from sorrow, toil, and pain, and sin we shall be free .... what Child is this.... as for me and my house .... I am dying .... *pain within my gut* .... I am living .... why? .... into Thy hands .... ninety-three .... the boy, oh God, the boy .... he cannot come to me .... sweet sentence gives .... Lord, now lettest .... when I thirst a mighty fortress .... that's a beautiful trillium .... the hound .... depart in peace .... amen .... alleluia .... six .... peace .... according to .... to Thy Word .... to Thy .... let Thy .... let Thy .... let Thy .... holy angel .... be .... be .... be .... with me .... with me .... Jude .... oh .... hey .... ah .... 'kay...."

That it was a sunny Wednesday afternoon, about 3:00pm, or that it was a day in January made no difference to the old man. Since the day was as the night to him, the marking of days and the passage of time remained unrecorded and unimportant.

The sound he heard instantly opened a door from the beginning of his days, one long closed in his mind, a noise not heard since the earliest of his years. That primal sound stilled the old man. His mind sharpened as intently as ever and his attention focused as it had many years ago. The old man, while the ancient rite took over, turned his glazed eyes to the wall at the foot of his bed. His darkened eyes focused on the panel of light and followed it as the journey to the corner of the room slowly commenced. Anticipation and fear rose and subsided instantly. Hope and good fear filled him. The reflection moved to the corner of the room. The grating sound came just as the old man expected. The cross-shadowed panel of light rushed to jump across the open doorway in the room.

Everything stopped at that moment, or rather, at that unmoment, for time had just intersected eternity. The light froze and, rather than jumping across the opening as it had done all the times before, it became fixed on the Ancient of Days who stood at and as the Doorway. Light came from that One. Pure light radiated from Him and revealed to the old man those who waited on the far side of the Doorway. He saw Gabby, the woman, the contender, the boy and a host of others.

Joy replaced worldly sorrow. Excitement supplanted all pains. Gladness vanquished despair. Mourning turned to dancing. Laughter evoked tears of joy. Instantly, not one of the other things had meaning or being. The casting of the old world's shadows no longer took place. Senses sharpened as never before during any part of the old life he once lived. Vitality displaced death. The former things passed away. Lungs inhaled as never before and the old man's heart pumped the blood of life. His ears, now tuned to perfection, heard the clear, thundering, welcoming voice of the Incarnate One.

"Well done. Come, little one, for all things are ready."

About the artist ...

Anisa L. Baucke has served as a teacher at the Evanjelicke Gymnasium (Lutheran High School) in the city of Tisovec of the Slovak Republic where she taught English and Art. She graduated from Concordia University in Seward, Nebraska in 1998 with a Bachelor of Science and Lutheran Teaching Diploma in Art Education K-12 and in Elementary Education. She is an artist in residence in Seward, Nebraska.

About the author ...

Michael L. McCoy has served as pastor of Our Redeemer Lutheran Church in Emmett, Idaho since 1984. In addition, he has served as missionary pastor of Shepherd of the Mountains Lutheran Church in Cascade, Idaho (1988-90), Word sower in Council, Idaho (1989) and vacancy pastor at Immanuel Lutheran Church in New Plymouth, Idaho (1994-96). Michael and Judy (nee Czech) have three children, Mary, Marji and Tony. He is a registered Professional Engineer in Oregon and has written *Creation vs. Evolution* (Concordia Publishing House, 1996) and *The Bestman, the Bride and the Wedding* (Clinton H. Jones Publishing, 1998).

In the several weeks prior to this manuscript being delivered to the publisher, there were two on-going episodes that confirmed one of the main themes of this book, the enduring efficacy of God's Word. Both visiting the sick and reading books are routine parts of a pastor's activities in the congregation. Ordinarily this would not be worthy of a reference here, however the particular parishioner I visited in recent weeks and the specific book I read do warrant mention for the purposes of encouraging you and yours to read good books and to be in the Word.

Carl is a member of the congregation I serve. He had serious health problems and if he did not undergo heart surgery in the immediate future, the 83-year-old man had about a year to live. The longer he waited, the greater his risk of not surviving the surgery. His weakened body and frail lungs increased the complications. Desiring to live and willing to die, Carl arranged to have the surgery and commended himself into the hands of God Who works through surgeons, nurses, technology and medicines to perform miracles. He survived the successful operation but his recovery was difficult and uncertain. In the first days after surgery, his heart had to be shocked into a regular rhythm. He remained intubated for a couple weeks before being trached and peg'd for several more weeks. While in intensive care, he could see reasonably well and, even without his hearing aids, could hear a bit. However, he was not able to speak. In the first weeks after his surgery, conversation with him remained impossible.

Six weeks after his operation we began to talk again. Since his situation was similar to the man in this book, I asked him what he thought about and what occupied his mind during those times when he could not speak or communicate with anyone.

The following is his answer, which is a compilation of several of our visits. I read the following conversation to him and he has indicated that it is accurate. I asked and received approval from him to include it in this after word.

"Carl, in the first weeks when you were in intensive care, were you aware of what was going on?"

"No, not really. Oh, I could tell when people were working on me. I could see and hear some, but people had to be close to me. If my mind was clear, I could think; but not concentrate for long. I couldn't talk or communicate with anyone. That was hard."

"Frustrating?"

"Oh yes."

"Was it like you were alone; with just you and the Lord?"

"Yes. What else was there? I couldn't talk to anybody."

"Tell me what you thought about during those times."

"I prayed, but they were not long prayers. I thought about God, my wife, my family and about what was happening to me, and why. I thought a lot, but I have to tell you, pastor, my thoughts were not always good thoughts. I questioned God and wondered why I was still here and why I suffered like this. I don't know what God wants me to do. I don't know what I will be able to do. I am so weak and I don't think I will be able to do anything. The improvement was so slow and I questioned God. Some were good thoughts, I think; but some thoughts were not good."

"Jesus had good thoughts for you and paid the price for all of your sins, including your bad thoughts, when He suffered on the cross. Do you believe this?"

"Yes, pastor."

"Carl, you are forgiven."

"Thank you, pastor. ... You know, when I was in the hospital and couldn't talk, I remember singing an old hymn in German in my mind. It was from a hymnal that my Uncle Bill, my father's brother, gave me when I was young. The hymn had words in it like God spreading His wings over me. But I couldn't remember all the words and I think I got them mixed up. You know, I'm not like you ministers who know where many things are in the Bible. I just know a few Bible verses that I keep repeating and thinking about I don't know where they are at in the Bible. When I was little it was the wish and will of my parents that I went to church. I have to tell you, there were many times I didn't see much use in it. I went to catechism class and was confirmed and I still didn't see what good it did me. Later in life though, I see where it helped. The hymns and Bible verses come back to me and I thought about these things. I sang the hymns in my mind and recited verses. God has been so good to me. But pastor, I think I am preaching to you. Should I be preaching to the preacher?"

"Yes, and Carl, what you are saying is extremely helpful."

"Really? How?"

"Well, a pastor teaches year after year. Classes are taught to people of all ages. Memory work is assigned to the kids in the church. They often complain about it and sometimes their parents do as well. People are encouraged to read and memorize the Word of God and the hymns of the Church. Sermons are preached each week, sometimes two or three times a week. Pastors know that the LORD God has promised that His Word will accomplish His purpose, but always according to His time table and not ours. Because pastors are sinful people, we are impatient, we complain and our thoughts aren't always good ones either. But every once in a while, the LORD encourages us by allowing us to see the fruits of another pastor's work from long ago. That is what I have been blessed to hear from you during our visits. In my visits with you, I have received as much from you, as you have from me."

"Do you, pastor?"

"Yes, and especially at this time."

"Why is that?"

"Well Carl, one reason is that I have written a book and am just getting it ready for the publisher. The man in the book underwent awful suffering just as you have. In our visits, you have told me about the experiences, thoughts, prayers and questions in your mind when it was just your Lord and you. You have confirmed what God says about His Word and that what I have written in the book is true."

"Really?"

"Yes, Carl, and there's something else."

"What's that, pastor?"

"As it is now written, I have four blank pages at the end of the book. That seems such a waste to me. So here's a question for you, Carl."

"What is it?"

"Do you think that a couple reasons why God wanted you to live and permitted you to suffer as you did was that, first of all, so you could tell me about your struggles that I might be encouraged; and secondly, so I might write your story on those four blank pages that others might be encouraged?"

"I don't know, pastor. It could be."

"Carl, would you give me permission to do just that?"

"Yes."

"I will write it and read it to you. If I have gotten anything wrong then you can correct me. Does that sound okay to you?"

"Yes."

"Carl, what would it have been like if you didn't have the Bible verses, the liturgy or God with you?"

"Oh, it would have been unbearable. There would have been no one with me. It would have been awful and horrible."

Wolf Larson is a wretched human being and a character who is easily hated and occasionally pitied. He is the heartless character in Jack London's 1904 work, *The Sea-Wolf*. Throughout this book, London permits the reader to peer into the mind of Wolf Larson. While the protagonist in *A Little One Amidst the Shadows* is assaulted by doubt as he remains faithful unto death, the antagonist in *The Sea-Wolf* is haunted with belief and finds it a fearful thing to fall into the hands of the living God.